Reflecting on
research practice

Reflecting on research practice

issues in health and social welfare

Edited by
Pam Shakespeare, Dorothy Atkinson
and Sally French

In collaboration with
Joanna Bornat, Ann Brechin, Sheila Peace,
Alyson Peberdy, Moyra Sidell, Jan Walmsley and
Fiona Williams

Open University Press
Buckingham · Philadelphia

Open University Press
Celtic Court
22 Ballmoor
Buckingham
MK18 1XW

and

1900 Frost Road, Suite 101
Bristol, PA 19007, USA

First Published 1993

A catalogue record of this book is available from the British Library

ISBN 0 335 19038 3 (pb)   0 335 19039 1 (hb)

Library of Congress Cataloging-in-Publication Data
Reflecting on research practice/ edited by Pam Shakespeare, Dorothy
Atkinson, Sally French.
    p.   cm.
Includes bibliographical references and index.
ISBN 0–335–19039–1 (hard)   ISBN 0–335–19038–3 (pbk.)
1. Social sciences–Research.   2. Sociology–Research.
I. Shakespeare, Pam, 1948– .   II. Atkinson, Dorothy, 1945–
III. French, Sally.
H62.R375 1993
300'.72–dc20   93–1683
                                                        CIP

Typeset by Inforum, Rowlands Castle, Hants
Printed in Great Britain by Biddles Ltd, Guildford and King's Lynn

To the research subjects who feature in our studies, and to researchers everywhere involved in, or embarking on, similar endeavours.

Contents

Contents

Contributors

Dorothy Atkinson is a Senior Lecturer in the School of Health, Welfare and Community Education. Her background is in social work and social work education and includes several years' experience of working with people with learning difficulties. Her OU work has been primarily in the learning disability field.

Joanna Bornat is a Lecturer in the School of Health, Welfare and Community Education who has worked on courses on ageing and community care. She is an editor of the Journal *Oral History*.

Ann Brechin lives with her husband and family in Milton Keynes. Previously a clinical psychologist, she has worked at the Open University for fourteen years with a particular focus on learning disability. She is a Senior Lecturer and currently Sub-Dean (Courses) in the School of Health, Welfare and Community Education.

Sally French is a physiotherapist with academic qualifications in psychology and sociology. She is actively involved as a researcher and writer in disability studies.

Sheila Peace is a Lecturer in the School of Health, Welfare and Community Education. Previously she was Senior Research Officer, and a founder member of CESSA at the University of North London. She has been involved in a wide range of research with older people particularly in the area of residential care.

Alyson Peberdy is a Lecturer in Health and Social Welfare at the Open University. She has research interests in disability, dying and the experience of ethnic minorities.

Pam Shakespeare has been a Lecturer in both Community Education and Health and Social Welfare at the Open University and worked on courses on ageing, health education and practice-related issues. In addition to conversation analysis she is interested in issues surrounding the development of accessible open learning materials.

Moyra Sidell is a Research Fellow and Lecturer in the Department of Health and Social Welfare at the Open University, with research interests in women's health, the health of older people, alcohol misuse, and death and dying.

Jan Walmsley is a Course Manager at the Open University. She took a degree in history after leaving school, and came to social research relatively late in life. Her ambition is to combine the strengths of history and sociology in her research and writing.

Fiona Williams is a Senior Lecturer in the School of Health, Welfare and Community Education at the Open University. She has written widely on social policy. She is on the editorial board of *Critical Social Policy* and in 1993 was Visiting Professor in Women's Studies at the Queen's University of Belfast.

Acknowledgements

We should like to thank Serena Stewardson for her patience in word processing and styling the drafts for this book, and the staff at Open University Press for their help and support.

Introduction

Dorothy Atkinson and Pam Shakespeare

This book explores and charts some of the hidden and unexplained aspects of work in social welfare research. It does this through the personal experience of ten researchers from a variety of social science and humanities disciplines reflecting upon their own place, thoughts and dilemmas in research work. The book reveals those aspects of research which usually remain concealed and undiscovered. The revelation of those hidden-from-view areas of research involves the book's authors in a process of *self-disclosure* and *self-reflection*. We disclose and reflect upon the place of the self in the development of ideas; in the setting up and the doing of research, including the building of research relationships; and in the processes of interpretation and dissemination. As authors we draw on our personal experience to develop behind-the-scenes and backstage accounts of what *really* happened (often in our lives as well as in our research) and to share the mistakes and the gaffes that occurred along the way.

The audience

In 'reflecting on research' in this book, we aim to engage the reader in a similar process of reflection. In revealing the hidden processes of research, and in disclosing our own personal doubts and dilemmas, we aim to connect with the reader's own experience. This experience may be research-related but, just as important, is real-life experience as a person, a practitioner or a client in the health and welfare field. In reflecting on our accounts, we hope that the reader will find connecting links with our experiences, and will find those connections at once supportive and reassuring. Doing research can be a lonely business: this book aims to reduce that sense of alone-ness.

The book is designed to appeal to people interested or involved in research at all levels. Thus it is meant for the beginning researcher, and the novice just setting out on research, who can benefit directly from reading, and taking heed of, other people's personal accounts; but it is also intended for more experienced or established researchers who can identify with the authors' doubts and dilemmas. In writing honestly, personally, and we hope accessibly, we also intend to demystify research. In doing so, we aim to engage a range of people who may have an interest in research, but who do not (yet) see themselves as researchers. This includes those who are merely curious and interested in research ideas and practice, as well as those who are, or have been, involved as subjects, respondents or participants. But we also aim to engage practitioners as researchers. In demystifying research, and in revealing the nature of much face-to-face research practice with individuals and groups, we intend to encourage practitioners to be reflective about their own practice and to think how research – their research – might improve or enhance their practice. This book is thus intended for reflective practitioners as well as reflective researchers.

The nature of the group

All the authors are women with a particular interest in exploring the lives and experiences of marginalized and oppressed groups in society. Some of us had already worked together on courses about learning disability and began to meet as a small informal research group interested in the possibility of participative research with people with learning disabilites. Gradually a wider group (the Reflective Research Group) formed, bound together by a mutual interest in research with marginalized or oppressed groups of people.

As we have written our various chapters it has become clear that our personal autobiographies are, in some sense, an important component of what we have to say. As draft material developed, a personal revelation on one person's part would often lead other people into (re)discovering the relevance of their own experience in relation to the research process. Also important is the fact that, roughly speaking, we are a cohort of white, middle-aged women whose academic background originated in the social sciences or humanities of the 1960s and 1970s and whose continuing involvement with the academic world has been set against a context of the changing philosophies and trends of social science. But, like most cohorts, in addition to our commonalities we represent a wide range of diversities in our social and personal backgrounds, and we have assimilated the influence of social scientific thinking and traditions in very different ways.

Our collaboration on the book has also been shaped by the collaborative mode of working, common at the Open University, where much of our work becomes the object of scrutiny by our fellow course team members. Everyone has read and commented on all the drafts of the material for this book. This way of working can be traumatic, but it can be very liberating too, in that we have regular opportunities to discuss the hidden processes of writing and to make connections with other people. The loneliness of the writing process is taken seriously at the Open University (although not always ameliorated) and does have parallels with the loneliness of research (and is, of course, in itself an aspect of the research process).

Inevitably in looking at ourselves – and our ideas, values and dilemmas – we also look reflectively at the *people* of whom we write, and with whom we work. Part of the legitimation for conducting our research, and for writing this book, is our commitment to improving *practice*. As health and social welfare researchers and writers (and in some instances, health and welfare professionals, too) this means not only highlighting good research practice but also striving for a positive impact on policy and practice within the field.

The book has three main areas of interest: it focuses on the *self* in research; the *subjects* of that research, the people who are written about; and *practice*, in its broadest sense. The book's themes are subsumed within these broad areas.

The research context

This book forms part of a developing literature of reflective research accounts. (See, for example, the collections compiled by Reason and Rowan 1981; Roberts 1981; Bowles and Duelli Klein 1983; Bell and Roberts 1984; Burgess 1984; Smith and Kornblum 1989; Ely et al. 1991; Gluck and Patai 1991; Steier 1991; Walford 1991.) The three main areas of interest in this volume echo and build on, indeed reflect, the work of others. There is agreement amongst many social researchers that knowledge is socially and culturally constructed (see, for example, Ravn 1991; Steier 1991). This means that the *researcher*, and the researcher's actions, are part of that process and should therefore be subject to self-reflection (see, for example, Duelli Klein 1983; Kornblum 1989; McCormack Steinmetz 1991). Knowledge is co-produced, involving the researcher *and* the researched (Reason and Rowan 1981; Gergen and Gergen 1991), where possible as co-researchers (Heron 1981). Research projects which involve people who are part of a subordinate social group or oppressed or otherwise vulnerable, raise ethical issues about the justification for doing research and have implications for how we carry out our work in practice (see, for example, Oakley 1981; Patai 1991; Stacey 1991).

The structure of the book

The order of the book is roughly in the chronological order of a research project, beginning with thinking and ending with the telling of research. The chapters are 'Thinking' by Fiona Williams, 'Negotiating' by Sheila Peace, 'Explaining' by Jan Walmsley, 'Observing' by Alyson Peberdy, 'Relating' by Dorothy Atkinson, 'Sharing' by Ann Brechin, 'Presenting' by Joanna Bornat, 'Performing' by Pam Shakespeare, 'Interpreting' by Moyra Sidell and 'Telling' by Sally French. We could have organized the chapters in a different way, for example, clustering them around intellectual traditions, organizational interactions and personal performances. But this would have undermined two elements that we think are important: the notion of research as having a process and as having a story. We know that the processes we have explored can take place at different stages in the research process and that researchers go through many cycles of negiotiating and explaining throughout their research. However we have chosen to juxtapose the many truths of research in a specific order that constitutes one particular story.

The ordering of the book is overlaid by the fact that we have all found our own ways of writing about our own experiences. The process unfolded in the book is not a seamless web because the process of writing the book has been a further story for us as a group of individuals in unearthing the hidden processes of research and connecting our own experience to that of other members of the group. The story has many resonances.

The themes

This section deals in turn with the three main areas of interest: the self; the research subjects; and practice.

The self

Our stance is reflective and biographical. Both individually and collectively we, as authors, are engaged in the personal and complex task of looking back on, and making sense of, not only our research endeavours but also our own lives. We thus include *autobiographical* accounts of ourselves as authors and, in turn, our accounts – often *biographical* – of the people whose views we sought and whose lives we documented.

This book is, therefore, about the use of self in research and writing and, at the same time, is a reflection on that use of self. It is a circular process (Ely et al., 1991; Steier 1991). The self, the 'I', is part of writing and research, and interacts with ideas and people. But 'I' can also stand back and reflect critically on that process. We reflect on the self in relation to our work in this volume in two main ways. We chart the origin and development of ideas, experience and knowledge through, for example, the recounting of a personal journey. (Several authors do this, but the most comprehensive example is Fiona Williams' autobiographical account). Elsewhere, we reflect on the use of self in research through the retrospective reconstruction of the life history of a research project. (An extended example of this process is provided by Moyra Sidell).

In writing about the use of self we are inevitably involved in a process of *self-disclosure*. Evidence of this is seen, in different ways, in all the book's accounts. An autobiographical account is, by its nature, a disclosure of some personal aspects of one's own life. But self-disclosure is also consciously used here in interviews, as a means of establishing rapport and creating the 'right' atmosphere to enable interviewees to disclose aspects of their own life histories. (See, for example, Jan Walmsley's account of finding the ways and means of explaining her research project to the people concerned). And the accounts of mistakes, misunderstandings, doubts and other personal mishaps which abound in the pages of this book are in themselves a very real form of self-disclosure. (There are many examples, but Sally French discloses a very personal account of the pressures and pitfalls of getting research published).

In many ways the authors of this book are involved in a process of developing *self-awareness*; an awareness of the influence, and use, of self in a research situation. This means, for some people, acknowledging their responsibility for the overall quality and integrity of their research, and for safeguarding the anonymity, confidentiality and general welfare of the research subjects.

The research subjects

An awareness of one's self is important in research; but, equally important, is an awareness of the 'subjects' of one's research. This *other-awareness* is reflected throughout the book in various ways. We use different terms to describe the people we write about and/or involve in our research projects. Some authors write simply about people, women and men, and families, whilst others distinguish race as an aspect of this other-awareness; some authors variously refer to participants, subjects and interviewees; and elsewhere more specific references are made to 'people with learning difficulties', 'disabled people', 'older women' and 'people with confused speech'.

The subjects of our research/writing are drawn primarily from oppressed, marginalized and otherwise vulnerable groups in this society. Authors testify to the importance, in this context, of developing an awareness of the potentially exploitative nature of face-to-face research. Other-awareness is a first step towards sensitive interviewing and an empathetic approach. This process is enhanced by our real-life experiences as women writers/researchers who have struggled for recognition in a predominantly male academic world. An awareness of otherness is thus an important second step in the development of good research practices. An understanding of our own experience of oppression and marginalization at least makes it possible for us to empathize with other people's experience in similar – and indeed very different – circumstances.

As authors we seek separately, and to some extent collectively, to justify the research we do in the health and social welfare area. The *legitimation* of our research is through the values we hold, and which underpin our work. The notion of *reciprocity* is considered important in this context; and we variously describe reciprocal interactions, shared endeavours (in producing a book or video, for example) and our stance as a 'friend', a 'confidante', a 'benefactor' or a 'scribe'. (Joanna Bornat, for example, describes how she has developed an awareness over the years of the mutual shaping of interviews by both parties). Second, we share a commitment to reducing the power differential in research settings through involving people as participants and – where possible – as active and equal partners. A participative approach to research means not only challenging the social divisions of gender, class, race, disability and age but also challenging the traditional professional–client differentiation in health and welfare settings (Sheila Peace, for example, looks back on her own research career to understand more about the researcher's position of relative power). Third, we seek to 'give a voice' to people otherwise rarely heard through documenting their (previously neglected or misrepresented) lives and experiences. (Several authors stress this: Dorothy Atkinson explicitly sets out to 'give a voice' to people with learning difficulties.) The legitimation of our research lies in its potential to empower the people about whom we write and with whom we research. (This point is made particularly strongly by Ann Brechin in describing her attempts to share the ownership of her research with the people involved.)

Practice

This book is grounded in practice. It is written by people who are research practitioners and, in several instances, also health/welfare practitioners, and it reflects therefore many of the dilemmas experienced by people in practice everywhere. It looks realistically at the challenges and the pitfalls, for example, of developing collaborative working and aiming for reciprocity in relationships.

'Practice' here refers both to the doing of research and to its effects. As authors we reflect at length on the doing of research. We look at research encounters, our interactions with subjects and at the building of research relationships. To a greater or lesser extent, we draw on previous and current personal/interactive/communication or other human skills (as a counsellor, a psychologist, a social worker, a nurse or a physiotherapist, for example) in the conscious use of self in research settings. These skills require self-awareness and the capacity to be introspective and reflective, (Pam Shakespeare, for example, looks honestly and critically at how she performs in her own research interactions).

The doing of research, in the context of this book, is not fixed, predictable or predetermined. Authors here approach their work in a spirit of openness, even uncertainty, about its likely course and direction. Part of the research process, as we see it, is the need to negotiate meanings with subjects and allow frameworks for understanding to evolve through time. Reality is neither entirely fixed nor given for all time. The use of self – the influence/impact of self – plays an important part in the unfolding of multiple realities. In this sense, research becomes part of a shared enterprise or a joint search for truth; a co-production of knowledge. (In this context Alyson Peberdy reflects on how the people she lived with and observed were actively involved in shaping and guiding her work.)

Active participation in research can, and does, lead to active participation outside research. Involvement in research often means people having an opportunity to recount their lives and experiences. Recounting is, necessarily, a self-reflective process and may lead to important changes. People may well, through reflection, develop insight and awareness, an enhanced sense of self and, perhaps, some useful self-advocacy skills. Research may thus bring about changes in practice, changes which continue long after the research project which inspired them is over. Examples in this book include people contributing to 'quality' groups in residential homes, developing self advocacy skills and participating in community oral history projects. In the context of recent legislation – in particular, the Children Act 1989 and the NHS and Community

Care Act 1990 – we hope that this book will also have an impact on the development of 'good practices' (for example, user participation and involvement) in the health and social welfare field.

Traditions and context

Having outlined what we consider to be the context of our research we want now to look at its provenance. In exploring this we want to acknowledge that there are both implicit and explicit aspects to this provenance. Some of us have drawn upon socialist and feminist traditions, scholarship and discourse to frame the problems we pose (Joanna Bornat, Fiona Williams), others have cited an array of individual influential twentieth century sociologists of various orientations ranging from Evans-Pritchard to Goffman to Foot Whyte (Alyson Peberdy, Pam Shakespeare and Jan Walmsley for example). Research concerns have also focused on the interplay between quantitative and qualitative research (Sally French, Sheila Peace, Moyra Sidell), on oral history (Dorothy Atkinson, Joanna Bornat, Jan Walmsley), the relationship between intellectual traditions and personal scholarship (Moyra Sidell and Fiona Williams) and the nature of subjects and objects in research and how we relate to interviewees as informants – those people who provide our data (Alyson Peberdy, Ann Brechin, Joanna Bornat, Dorothy Atkinson, Pam Shakespeare, Jan Walmsley). It seems to us, however, that there are broader and often implicit contexts in which our work can be placed, although this varies from author to author. The fact that we try to deal with the notion of representing many voices in a research context (our own voice as well as the voices of our subjects, funders, publishers, other theorists and practitioners), together with our emphasis on uncertainties and dissonance within the research role, and the values we place on the variety of subjective experience, all reflect a wider context in current social science debates.

First, the focus on participatory research is related to the feminist debate about the relationship of the researcher with her research subjects, which leads us to the question of the ability of the feminist researcher to be a 'knower' (Smith 1987) (a role traditionally denied to women, except that is, for wise women who have been seen as dangerous as much as knowing) without its attendant implications of power over her research subjects. Second, by contrast, the focus on marginalized and oppressed social groups relates to issues about empowerment, to the political implications of research and ultimately to questions about how autonomy, justice and equity can be construed in research. Third, the concern with self and other, subject and object as well as subject and subject of research, and the questions about the status of the 'voices' in the research these can all be placed in the context of the debate on postmodernism. Let us briefly consider these three debates.

In our espousal of participatory research we have drawn upon feminist scholarship and discourse to frame the problems we pose. Particularly we have been concerned with the place of the personal in the research process. Here we have conceived personal in a number of ways: as a mode of self description; as part of the process of theorizing; as part of a methodology – the person seen reflexively; and as a mode of evaluation. We implicitly challenge objectivism: 'a pathology of cognition that entails silence about the speaker, about his (sic) interests and his desires and how these are socially situated and structurally maintained' (Gouldner cited in Soderqvist 1991: 147). Instead we look to our own world and our own knowledge to throw light on what we are doing. As Dorothy Smith says:

> [the researcher] begins from her own original but tacit knowledge and from within the acts by which she brings it into her grasp in making it observable and in understanding how it works. She aims not at reiteration of what she already (tacitly) knows, but at an exploration through that of what passes beyond it and is deeply implicated in how it is.
>
> (Smith 1987: 92–3)

Well yes, we do want to take this book beyond tacit personal knowledge and explore how it is implicated in the research process but to do this in a way that is not exclusive and excluding. We have tried to write accessibly, and several authors have used devices to point this up, for example, Moyra Sidell has used a cartoon-like line drawing to clarify her model, and Fiona Williams has inverted the 'laws of writing' to this purpose by making her footnotes academic and the text personally focused. We want to be knowers, but what we know must be accessible to others, particularly those who provide us with our research data. It's a long step from theorizing and fighting your corner with an academic audience to embedding your research and its findings in a medium accessible to a wide audience as Sally French discusses in 'Telling'.

Picking up on this general theme of using the personal as a platform for research understanding, Stanley and Wise say:

> It has been suggested to us that what we are proposing is mere self indulgence. While rejecting the 'mere' we also believe that it is self indulgent to do anything other than we suggest. Most social science research, and most feminist research has been riddled with the self indulgences of people who have refused to face up squarely to their own active involvement within the central process of constructing research.
>
> (Stanley and Wise 1983: 197)

To this we would add that our autobiographies have had a role to play in the construction of our research. Our personal histories are germane to our conduct of research and construction of knowledge. Part of our aim has been to make our autobiographies of knowledge and research a little more conscious and explicit and a little less involuntary. (This point echoes Liz Stanley's argument in favour of the inclusion of the writer's 'intellectual autobiography' in biographical writing (Stanley 1992: 177).)

The issues of participatory research have an immediacy that is not apparent in all the contexts that have influenced us. These are issues about how we relate to other people, how much of ourselves we put into our research and so on. But our autobiographies are embedded in broad intellectual traditions too. To discover one is a postmodernist or a Cartesian dualist has, for some of us at least, been congruent to the joke about the woman who discovered she's been talking prose all her life. For others the debate surrounding postmodernism had previously been embraced as part of their intellectual persona. It is in these broader contexts that we perhaps show our diversities more than in other areas we have outlined earlier.

Whether we like it or not we are all working in an intellectual climate which is postmodern, where we are uneasy about notions of truth and where knowledge is always questionable. This strikes at the heart of the research enterprise; after all, arguments between quantitative and qualitative research methodologies were about how you could best gain access to the truth. If we no longer search for the 'truth', or even some approximation of it, what are we doing? Many of our chapters reflect this uncertainty. We have found it both liberating and chastening at the same time. It has allowed us to challenge 'objectivity', to let ourselves in on the act, to be partial and to put forward the view from the standpoint of women, older people, people with learning disabilities and so on.

The process of collaboration

The preparation of this book has been through a process of collaboration. As a consequence, the book is not only an expression of a collaborative way of working, it is also an embodiment of the group's commitment to be openly – and honestly – reflective about being a researcher and doing research.

The book is distinctive, then, not only in its content but also in its production, for it has been produced by a process of drafting – reflection – re-drafting. The reflective process itself thus became part of the production process and operated at both individual and group levels. On an individual basis the very act of writing about research involved each of us in standing back from, and making sense of, the processes involved in our work. The additional group discussion and feedback loops added new dimensions – and insights – to the ideas, interpretations and explanations of individual authors. The finished product has been enriched by the two interacting layers of reflection.

At an individual level, each author has reflected on the place of her self in her own research. Thus, for example, in writing about observing in research the reflective process involved Alyson Peberdy, the author, in standing back and observing her self as an observer. Similarly, in reflecting on performing Pam Shakespeare, the author, temporarily joins the audience to witness her own performance from the overture to the final curtain.

At a group level authors have written, and circulated for comment, three sequential drafts of their chapters, and each version of each chapter has been discussed by the group. The group has been both supportive and challenging, and has had a major impact on how the final accounts now look. Feedback from colleagues has led to changes in language, content and (self) understanding. As the shared endeavour was all about revealing the hidden aspects of the research process, the group has played its part by providing the inspiration, the encouragement, and even the permission for people to disclose what really happened in their research and, often, in their lives. The result is that some of the authors have revealed far more about their research, and themselves, than they might otherwise have dared to do.

The chapters of this book represent the individual accounts of our research and writing. But the book is more than the sum of its individual parts. It represents a collective stance and is a reflection of a group effort. Taken as a whole, this book is itself an example of qualitative research, in that it documents the ideas, lives and experiences – some personal and some research-based – of a group of women researchers. It is an approach which can easily be replicated and we hope that other groups of researchers will take up the challenge to be openly reflective about their own work.

Of course, in saying we have written about hidden aspects of research we have not even now told the whole story. The drafting process has helped organize and articulate our thoughts but in so doing has re-hidden some of the thoughts and ideas unearthed in earlier stages. Some aspects remain hidden and unarticulated now. The whole research process is a selective process. We are aware that in our final choice of a 'storyline' we have presented a partial story. Nevertheless, as we tell our stories, we become aware that each story is only one among many. Dorothy Atkinson, Joanna Bornat, Ann Brechin and Jan Walmsley are particularly concerned with whose story carries weight. Alyson Peberdy portrays a situation where she couldn't get access to the story she wanted because she was an outsider (albeit of a dominant world group) and a woman in the society in which she was working. Moyra Sidell juggles several different stories together. Sheila Peace and Sally French explore what story to tell to whom. These could have been different stories completely. As we become aware of this we open up to an awareness that our research subjects do that to us – tell us one story among many.

1

Thinking
Exploring the 'I' in ideas

Fiona Williams

When ideas for this book were floated I felt enthusiastic but sceptical. I recognized that focusing largely upon experiential accounts of different aspects of the research process would help demystify and assert some important principles and ethical concerns, but I was worried that it might be rather self-indulgent. This worry reflects partly my struggle to develop new ideas and write them, for this involves a battle between an intense self-doubt which says that those ideas are not of sufficient importance or coherence to be written down or read, and an equally intense and driven conviction that I have something insightful and important to say. Indeed, the very act of getting it written down is an exhausting but exhilarating process whereby the conviction overcomes, or at least holds at bay, the self-doubt. However, to write about that process and not the end product of the ideas themselves – the 'I' in ideas – filled me with even greater self-doubt. People may want to read my ideas, but are they really interested in how and from where they have emerged, especially as it is so difficult to present this in a systematic fashion? Is it possible, in academic terms, to write about the relationship between personal experience and theoretical thinking (some might call it 'the mode of intellectual production') in a way that demystifies, reassures other writers, and does not vaunt or reify that particular experience?

After several attempts at developing these ideas, I decided to interview myself in writing. At first this was mainly an intuitive move – it seemed to provide the possibility of representing in an accessible way the accidental and fragmentary nature of epistemological experience. Subsequently I realized it had greater significance.[1] Traditionally social sciences literature has created a distance between the academic's own life and her material (there are exceptions, of course, and this book fits into such a stream). To close that distance smacks of self-indulgence. Yet to exclude it is to ignore some of the important specifics and dynamics of intellectual resource material.[2] The only way I could allow myself to tell a personal story was to turn myself into a research subject whose personal intellectual development becomes the object of inquiry by a researcher: a shifting from subject to object to subject.[3] I also decided to partially invert the normal academic convention where items of personal observation and detail are relegated to footnotes. Here, the substantive text carries the personal story and the footnotes indicate academic references and discussions.

In my struggle for the 'right' to write, I often lighten the sense of responsibility by telling myself I am only a scribe, a representative interpreter of social life in a specific time and place. I am the clerk in the courtroom. All that happened was that as I grew up someone handed me a pen and said, 'Take the minutes.' Yet, at the same time, I know I bring to my writing the accumulation of personal experience. My ideas are representative of who and what I am within a certain time and place, and they are only original in so far as they fuse together an individual perception and interpretation, which is shaped by both personal history and social location, with a shared social, political and cultural experience.

The aim of the interview is to use autobiography to explore some of these hidden dynamics behind the production of academic text. Three aspects are developed: the interconnected personal and political relationship to a field of knowledge (social policy); the struggle to acquire legitimacy as an academic writer; and the actual process of writing.

Q. *This chapter is called 'Thinking'. What do you mean by that?*

A. It's about what influences researchers to make sense of the world in the way that we do – what is behind the theories, explanations, the analyses and the concepts that we use in our research. There is a strong argument which says that it is important to acknowledge personal experience, in terms of your location in society, as a lens through which you make sense of the world and reshape existing knowledge. For instance, Dorothy Smith says that women social scientists are often forced to reorganize sociological knowledge to make it work for their experience. For her it is women's direct experience of the everyday world which is the necessary starting point for developing an alternative knowledge. The same argument can be applied to other oppressed or marginalized groups – working-class people, black women and men, gay men and lesbians, for example.[4]

But I also take thinking to include the process of communicating understanding, in this case through writing – the creation of the academic product, if you like. We all try to make sense of our world, but not everyone writes it down. The development of one's identity as a writer – what I call acquiring the right to write – and the intensely (usually) individual process of writing are little discussed in research manuals. They are central yet taken-for-granted aspects of the research process.[5]

Q. *Perhaps we can come back to that. First, what do you write about?*

A. My field is social policy, but a lot of my written work has involved examining the relevance of social theory to the study of welfare and vice versa.[6] However, since 1988 I've worked at the Open University, and that means that most of my teaching centres upon producing distance learning materials which involves collaborative writing.[7]

I'm interested in the conceptual challenges that theories of oppression and liberation pose for social theory in general and for our understanding of welfare in particular. I think that those theories around class, gender, 'race', disability, sexuality and age which have stemmed from an active engagement with these as areas of oppression have influenced and changed the ways we think about welfare and the ways we research it. (Of course those theories themselves have also undergone considerable change.) My writing has attempted to chart and evaluate these processes. But this hasn't been simply an intellectual exercise, because in different ways I have lived through these changes too.

Q. *What do you mean 'lived through'?*

A. Well, like many people, especially women, I can't represent my life in a unilineal way, but more as a mosaic or patchwork of experiences and understandings picked up and added to or picked up and dropped, or picked up later, with certain themes running through. Also, it's possible to make sense of this patchwork in different ways: as a woman (white, English), as an activist, as a writer, as an academic, as a member of a particular generation, as a mother, in terms of the first ten years, or the last ten, or in terms of close relationships. I'll use some, not all, of these here.[8]

One obvious place to begin is university where I went to study social administration with sociology in 1965. Like many of that post-war generation, first in our families to experience higher education, I was intellectually eager and thirsty for new ideas. So I was quite disappointed with what I was presented. Social administration was, quite literally, about the administration and implementation of social policies. There was little that linked it to sociology or social theory except perhaps concepts of poverty and deprivation. It was overwhelmingly empirical and descriptive. I learned to understand how policies worked, but not to make sense of them as part of a world I experienced. Nor did I find out much about what these policies might mean to the people for whose benefit they were intended. Social administration's standpoint, rarely articulated, was that of a Fabian policy-maker, and insofar as it engaged with action, this was social work. That's not to say it wasn't interesting, it's just that it seemed to have little personal or political relevance to the world outside the lecture-room doors. This was, after all, London in the period leading up to the student rebellions of 1968, where you could take your pick from class struggle, anti-imperialism, revolutionary change, sex, drugs and rock'n'roll, and even the faint stirrings of a women's movement.

Not surprisingly, after getting my degree, I dropped Social Administration. Instead I picked up a Commonwealth Scholarship and went to Nigeria to study the impact of imperialism and westernization upon West African women. The interest in imperialism picked up threads elsewhere in my life. My very early childhood was spent in Cairo where my father was an engineer, and my earliest political experience was his arguments against British intervention in Suez in 1956. I also had a long and complicated relationship with a Pakistani postgraduate student, which taught me a great deal, not least about racism, Islam, Marxism and sexual politics.

The research was a good idea, but it was the wrong time and maybe the wrong researcher. Radical sociologists in West Africa were interested in the potential of the developing working class. Political scientists were interested in the Black Power movement. Those interested in social change focused on urbanization and industrialization. I was interested in all of these, but at that time none of them had a place for, or an analysis of, women or domestic life. Those interested in women were anthropologists, who were more concerned with kinship and residence patterns than with power. I fell between several stools without the intellectual capital to pick myself up.

Back in London in the early 1970s, with my notes towards a thesis in two black and gold Biba bags (where they still remain) I found myself back in Social Administration, this time teaching it at North London Polytechnic. Here I was absorbed into a world in which the job of teaching sociology and social administration to health and welfare professionals was just one part of revolutionary praxis. At that time I, along with many of, if not most of my colleagues, was involved in revolutionary politics, mainly through the International Socialists. Our lives were a seamless web of intensely dedicated activities and duties for the cause. Our work, our politics, our leisure all overlapped to become scarcely distinguishable from each other. The routines of getting up early to sell papers outside a factory, giving lectures and seminars, organizing lunch-time meetings at work, developing radical broadsheets on welfare issues, going to trade union meetings and selling papers around council estates in the evenings all merged together. We were driven by a certainty that we were not only teaching history but making, indeed transforming, it too. We may not have been the central agents of this – for these were the organized working class – but we were prepared to put all our intellectual and organizational skills (which were considerable) to, as we believed, their benefit.

Q.   *What impact did this have on you?*

A.   In these unpredictable times it is more fashionable to parody and distance oneself from this sort of driven certainty than it is to recall its positives. It is true that we had a dogmatic arrogance, we disdained alternative ideas, and that, for many, the authority of certainty replaced the lack of authority and certainty elsewhere in our lives, and the certainty of that political authority undermined our individual thinking. Yet, at the same time, for me and for others, these were formative and important years. First of all, Marxism was the first theory that I learned in a non-academic way. I learned it not as a set of abstract ideas but as a theory which applied both to history and to the every-day events around me. It seemed to allow me to make sense of so much, for which up till then I had only discrete and partially-absorbed understandings – not only the political but the social and cultural and creative, too. It also gave me the conceptual tools to evaluate much (not all, as I came to realize) of life. The notion that our lives, their situations, events and histories could be understood in terms of contradictory forces which stemmed from an inherent conflict of interests between the working and capitalist classes was massively enlightening.

Second, the forms in which that knowledge was transmitted were important. I learned in discussion, argument and conversation with friends and comrades of all ages – people who could recount to me their involvement in the General Strike or the Spanish Civil War or the St. Pancras Rent Strikes. I learned in day schools, workshops, strike committees, over meals and in bed. Unlike school and university, knowledge was not an acquisition, a commodity, its understanding not marked by test or examination. Instead, I learned that knowledge was born of, and should be put to, the benefit of collective struggle, rather than the achievements of academics. Since at that time the organization had many members who were shop stewards and trade unionists without formal educational training, a premium was put on the passing on of ideas in an accessible way. Indeed, we ourselves were forced to learn that too, because you didn't last long at a factory gate or on the corridor of a windy high-rise if no one could understand what you were talking about. Of course there was a downside to all of this it led to a lot of mouthing of slogans and a fear of political 'incorrectness'.

Q. Did these ideas have any effect on your teaching of social administration?

A. Yes, quite a lot. In our teaching we began to question the Fabian idea of the welfare state as the apotheosis of social democratic redistribution. Instead, drawing on a small but growing literature, we presented an analysis of the welfare state as the result of an uneasy truce between capital and labour, improving but also controlling and disciplining the lives of the working class.[9] Since we were teaching welfare professionals, what became pressing was the need to develop strategies for those who found themselves working as 'agents of the state'. *Case-Con* – 'the magazine for revolutionary social workers' – emerged from our department. This developed the view that the job of the radical social worker was to develop trade union (rather than professional) consciousness and through that develop alliances with other trade unionists and support local collective action such as rent strikes, demands for childcare provisions or better benefits. Such a strategy faced internal contradictions which we were only beginning to appreciate. I was secretary of the Camden and Islington Public Sector Alliance at the time (during the major public sector strikes of 1972–74). In 1973 local DHSS counter staff, not noted for their radicalism, threatened strike action over pay. On the eve of the strike the Alliance met to find that the local

Claimaints' Union (who were also members of the Alliance) were urging suspension of the strike because it would hit families on benefit who were due to draw their benefit the next day. This had a knock-on effect for social workers who were supporting the strike but would be pressed to make Emergency Payments for the claimants. In addition, the Claimants' Union DHSS staff, striking or not striking, were the most oppressive people on earth. What we had imagined was the opportunity for class alliance and support merely exposed forms of conflict and distrust within welfare that we had hardly begun to make sense of.

Q.   *Where does feminism fit in to all this?*

A.   Well, in contrast to all this, I sort of transfigured towards the end of the 1970s and found myself living on an out of town estate in the South West with two children under two, unable to drive, with no job to return to, and doing boring traffic surveys to maintain the tiniest degree of economic independence. Like the conflict between the Claimants' Union and the DHSS staff, this was another aspect of my experience that Marxist theory or revolutionary practice didn't help to explain. (Also, how was it that my erstwhile male colleagues were all slipping into academic respectability or institutional security?)

Practically, personally and politically, feminism reached those parts that other theories couldn't. Feminist writings and activities also sharpened my understanding of social welfare issues. Added to this, before I had my children I had spent a year doing social work, and this had really exposed to me a dearth in my own skills and analysis and also in the lack of public provision to meet the needs of the women who were mainly my clients. I found, as well, that the professional culture at that time (and this was in the provinces, hardly touched by radical ideas) had a strange distorting effect on my understanding of human nature and human potential. I began to see people as the sum of their case-notes, which were usually catalogues of their deficits and deprivations. It seemed that if I could not make the transition in my own head from the idea of people as victims to people as agents of their own lives, I had little to offer them.

My involvement in feminist politics helped shift this a bit. Amongst other things, I was involved in the campaigns around abortion, setting up a local refuge for women and children escaping domestic violence and later a well-women's centre. Through these I became aware not only of the centrality of welfare provision in women's lives but also how we needed to take more seriously people's experiences of the way welfare agencies treated them/us. Our understanding of the negative side of this – the sexism, the racism – was still pretty limited. In the course of trying to get new forms of provision established, we also became more committed to the idea that relationships between users and providers did not have to be hierarchical and bureaucratic. These developments, and the desire to re-evaluate our understanding of what the welfare state meant, were reflected nationally. In 1980 the inaugural meeting of the journal *Critical Social Policy* – set up to 'break the mould of Fabian social administration' and develop a socialist and feminist approach to welfare – drew 1500 people. And, as Thatcherism began, the analysis of a so-called crisis of the welfare state became central to political, sociological and cultural studies analysts.[10]

Q. In terms of developing theory about the welfare state, how did these experiences influence your writing?

A. First, feminist analyses and campaigns threw new light on how we understood the welfare state, because they revealed some of the sexist underpinnings of provisions which we had up to then thought of as working-class victories. They also exposed the hidden, unpaid or low-paid contribution women made to welfare through caring and caring work. However, even as these analyses became more sophisticated and thorough, the mainstream of the discipline still tended to marginalize them.

Second, you had only to have been a member of a women's group for a few weeks to be aware (if not to talk about) that although the shared experiences of sisterhood and oppression were strengthening and bonding, there were also significant differences between women. There were differences in the way women experienced their oppression, in the strategies open to them to overcome it and in the way feminists explained it. In the early 1980s the most vociferous and appealing defence of the celebration of sisterhood in terms of women's special culture and values came from radical feminists, and I think the most coherent challenge to the so-called 'false universalism' of sisterhood came from Black feminists.[11] A lot of the experiences Black feminists pointed to were of the health, welfare and education services. (Later on in the 1980s the organization and writing of disabled feminists also called into question some of the earlier feminist assumptions about the universality of women's caring role).[12] At the same time, others in the 'race field' were painstakingly documenting examples of state racism, and this, far more than feminism, was being overlooked by the discipline of social policy (as it was now called).

Third, although the Marxist critique of welfare that we had been teaching at North London Poly now had a more refined rendering through the 'political economy of welfare', on the whole this critique only explained issues of gender and 'race' (if at all) in terms of the nature of production and the needs of capitalism.[13] Also, it was clear that the nature of the contradictions of welfare were different for women, and different for different groups of women, and these needed spelling out.

I felt that it was important to develop a more complex framework of analysis of welfare in which questions of gender and patriarchy and 'race' and imperialism, and the struggles around these, could be brought into focus with class/capital relations. Unless this was developed, social policy could go on being conceptualized and taught as though gender and 'race' were special-interest topics. I also thought that work in gender and 'race' had posed some theoretical challenges which social policy could benefit from thinking about.

Q. Such as?

A. For example, the fact that most analyses and programmes of welfare start by implicitly posing the question: 'What are the production needs of this society, and how is this organized, and how can we connect welfare provision up to that?' rather than, or as well as, 'What are the care needs in this society, and how is this organized, and how can we connect welfare provision up to that?' In short, the problem of economic determinism. There is also the problem of reductionism – explaining welfare policy in terms of a single cause , say, capitalism, or patriarchy.

Another problem that emerged with a lot of both radical and right-wing liberal thinking is the assumption of essentialism as a way of explaining difference.[14] Quite a lot of celebratory feminist politics implicitly confers a specialness to women that is born of their very nature – biological, psychic or whatever. Similarly some social reformist and right-wing theories justify women's confinement to domesticity in terms of some 'natural' or God-given characteristics. In the area of 'race' there have been similar developments in terms of Black or ethnic or cultural essentialism related to arguments about separate education and welfare provision. One of the intellectual responses to this has been to develop social construction theories – and this applies to other areas like age, disability and sexual orientation.[15] Of course, the danger here is that you can end up actually failing to acknowledge biological/physical/ cultural differences where they do have significance. I felt it was important not to deny differences but to emphasize that their significance is conditional upon the social and material conditions in which they exist.

Also, once you begin to explore questions of 'race' and racism in relation to welfare development, you get into a different analytical ball-game, because you need to understand welfare in terms of the changing nature of imperialism and the international movement of migrant labour.

Q. Were you influenced by anything else outside the discipline of social policy?

A. Before I embarked on developing these ideas, I had spent a year on an action-research project looking at education and employment opportunities for pupils in a working-class area of Plymouth. In searching to make sense of what the teachers, pupils and parents told me I came across a book called *Unpopular Education* (CCCS 1981). The analysis in that book really excited me. First, it took seriously popular consciousness and experience of education and used it as a starting-point of analysis; second, it attempted to integrate class and gender analyses; third, its historical analysis was dynamic – it set policies and the experiences of them within a specific set of historical and cultural conditions and showed how, often in a contradictory way, these shifted over time. That book came out of the Centre for Contemporary Cultural Studies at Birmingham University as did *The Empire Strikes Back* (1982), which was about 'race' and racism and which I also read closely. The analyses in these books had not only a dynamism but also a capacity to account for agents of resistance and social change beyond the rather restricted notion of class struggle.[16] However, not much of their work examined the welfare state.

Another important influence on me in the mid-1980s was my involvement in a research project comparing British and Hungarian welfare states. Over a period of several years two colleagues and I met up with three Hungarian counterparts. My visits to Hungary (for this was before liberalization) accompanying my colleagues on their research field trips, hearing their own life-histories and those of their interviewees, really forced me to rethink a lot of my earlier political education. Even though I had been part of the Trotskyist left which villified Stalinism and denounced the Soviet Union and Eastern Europe as 'state capitalist', I was aware that there was still a feeling on the left that these countries were nearer socialism than we were in the West. After all, there wasn't unemployment, most of the women even had paid work, and there were cheap restaurants and socialized childcare . . . All this and more was challenged by what I saw and heard. There were social conditions that shocked me, like dire poverty, which no one could document for fear of their livelihood being taken from them; there was the state oppression of the gypsy communities; there was the suppression of democratic forms; there was the state invasion of privacy and the consequent jealous guarding of close relations and family life (which rendered Western feminist ideas of oppressive family life strangely tangential even though relevant). But what shocked me more was that it had all taken place in the name of Marxism; the language of Marxism was the language of oppression. What I came to relearn was that Marxism could be a method, a critique, but it was not an ideology, a truth or an answer. It wasn't as though I didn't already know this, but I hadn't grasped it in my gut, as I did then. And this really applied to all the 'isms' in general. You could be, indeed it was important to be, an 'ist' with all your heart and soul, but you shouldn't let the 'ism' rule you. It may provide the guidelines but it should not rule you.

About this time I was beginning to write more for academic publication, and this realization was, in retrospect, an important factor in freeing me to have the right to write.

Q. You mentioned the right to write and tensions in the writing process at the beginning. Can you elaborate on this?

A. Yes, though it's quite a difficult knot to untangle. In 1984 I started work on what was to me then a *magnum opus*; a textbook in social policy that would present an integrated theoretical analysis of the welfare state in terms of race, gender and class. I completed it in 1987. The act of writing it required, more than anything, sustained courage. In fact, I think for many women academic writing – whether books or essays – is an act for which they should award bravery medals. You have to do it even though in so doing you feel you risk so much.

I think what I came to realize was this: that those struggles against the conditions which seemed to conspire to prevent me from writing actually contributed towards and drove me into writing. The imperative to write came from those experiences I have described – the discipline, as an academic, as a woman and so on. Those conditions were in effect the legitimation of my right to write. In other words, the tension between demoralizing self-doubt and driven conviction is almost necessary.[17] Sometimes this feels like a struggle between life and death itself. There was a time when I had a study where the desk faced a window which overlooked the road below, and I used to imagine, as I summoned up each morning the courage/confidence to write, that some force might hurl me through the window if I didn't get down what I wanted to say.

Q. *That sounds awful. Really?*

A. It sounds melodramatic, but it's true. Fortunately my desk now faces Velux windows, though there is a rather steep stairwell behind me . . . But that was at the beginnning. I now accept that from time to time, especially if I'm working on something new, this strange melodrama will be enacted in my head. And I understand it for what it is.

Q. *Which is?*

A. Well, at the time I wrote that book there were (and still are) a number of conditions which created enormous difficulties for me, or anyone else, to take myself seriously as an academic writer. First, for years I had been dodging and weaving between looking after my kids and part-time lecturing (sometimes in three different institutions one hundred miles apart) and short-term contracts – one-year at most. (Only in 1992 did I get, for the first time in 15 years, a permanent post). The Polytechnic where I did most of my teaching used me as a general dogsbody. Other staff (and these were mainly men) took sabbaticals, and I did their teaching. Of course in the process I learned a great deal, for example, the patchwork nature of my work-life turned me, of necessity, into an interdisciplinarian – an attribute I now regard as a positive virtue. I knew then that I had sufficient knowledge, but this wasn't reflected in institutional support, pay or status. I had no room, no secretarial support, no backing to go to conferences, no sabbaticals, of course, and little institutional encouragement or interest. But I did have personal encouragement from close friends; the discussions and arguments especially around gender and 'race' in the *Critical Social Policy* editorial group (of which I was and am a member) often crystallized my thinking; and the publishers had faith in me; that was important. Fortunately, too, after a couple of years I got a half-time research post (the Hungarian Experience).

Second, writing requires uncluttered time and space and to get that means putting your needs first. If you live in a household (and even if you don't) where people are used to you supporting their needs, or at least their access to you being constrained mainly by external factors like paid work or other domestic duties, this can be quite challenging. It's difficult too to find a rationale for such self and time-absorbing activity – its success is not guaranteed and there appear few tangible results to show. With endless negotiations over time and space, and with such apparent disruption to others' lives and the flow of family life, can it be really worth it? It's not just writing books that creates this scenario, mature women students doing undergraduate and post-graduate courses will be familiar with it. Either it paralyses you or you push through it and come out even more determined than ever to show yourself, and everybody else who has so much as squeaked a note of reservation, that it was really worth it. You can be driven under, driven crazy or driven to write.

These sorts of pressures and constraints also made me very disciplined and organized with my time, although I must say, I look forward to a time when I can be less pressured and less disciplined. When people sometimes say my writing is intense, I feel like explaining that that's usually because I have had to put it all down in three sentences before the children come home from school and my concentration is broken.

For me, two further things compounded the self-doubt. The first is that I write about theoretical work and, apart from feminist theory, this is largely the domain of men. When I read through all the existing general analytical works and textbooks in social policy, very few of them had been written by women. I kept thinking that it would have been safer to keep to something down-to-earth or to feminist theory alone. Added to this I wanted to challenge the discipline of social policy right down to its very Y-fronts. How absurd could you get!

The second aspect was this: enlightening and grounding as my involvement in political activity had been, it inhibited me. Part of me was still hung over with the idea that writing was a relative luxury and was using up energy that should really go into organizing. In addition another part of me was nervous about developing ideas that I knew transgressed the political orthodoxies – socialist and feminist – with which I was familiar. The experience of Hungary partly helped me overcome this, but in the end I simply had to learn to trust my intellectual and political integrity. And this I found extremely liberating.

A final issue was that though I felt I had the right to write about class and gender, had I, as a white woman, the right to write about 'race'? In fact, in the end, I felt quite strongly that it was important for me, as a white writer, to read what Black writers had to say, take on board their criticisms and apply these to my sphere of knowledge. (Had I been involved in developing primary research data, the issue would have been a bit different.)[18]

In so far as my self-doubt was partly drawn from my experiences as a woman in academia, then I think it has helped me in two ways. Standing (or even choosing to stand) on the margins of knowledge and the institutions of knowledge can give you an edge – a sensitivity or empathy to the writings and experiences of other 'others'. (This isn't necessarily the case though, and I would be cautious about assuming a transferability of experiences from one area of oppression to another). Second, if you are continually forced to justify the relevance of your standpoint from the perspective of mainstream thinking then you tend to build into your work a conscious, though unwritten, stream of self-criticism. As a result you become much more aware that what you write can never be the last word and this in itself can help you to be open to challenging ideas. I think I'm saying that it's possible to turn an internalized sense of subordination and marginalization to positive effect. But I would also say that being a woman is only one part of my being an academic writer. I have to go beyond who and what I am, yet also keep connected to it. I think that although I make sense of the world through a woman's eyes, the lens through which I look is quite a kaleidoscope of given and assumed identities. Having said that, I do feel that creating a piece of written work has similarities with giving birth – more a mode of reproduction than a mode of production. First there's a period of gestation, then the agony and ecstasy of birth, then you bond and after a bit you let go. And life goes on.

Q. *Are you still worried about the self-indulgence of this interview?*

A. A little, yes. Maybe footnotes will help.

Acknowledgements

I would like to thank John Clarke, Mary Langan and Anne Showstack Sassoon for their interesting and constructive comments on a second draft of this chapter.

Notes

1. I subsequently came across a very helpful paper by Anne Showstack Sassoon (1992) which argues eloquently for explorations into the subjective modes of intellectual work. She says 'I am convinced that what is experienced as an individual struggle about the nature and conditions of intellectual work today may have a wider resonance and that these questions should be on our agenda' (p.1). Mary Evans also develops an explanation and argument for the recent development of interest in biography in the social sciences. Postmodernism and individualism have given a new respectability to the individual and it is possible, she argues, to develop a new form of biography – social biography – which can throw new light on the old question of the relationship between the individual and society: 'The use of biography becomes not just to illustrate a social theory but to explain its meaning' (1992: 13). Only at proof reading stage did I get hold of Liz Stanley's wonderful exploration of these issues (Stanley 1992; see also the Special Issue of *Sociology* 1993).
2. Attempts to close the gap in the social sciences meet with profoundly different responses. Contrast, for example, two reviews in the same edition of *The Higher*, October 16th, 1992. In the first, a review of Peter Hennessy's book *Never Again Britain 1945–51* (1992), Nevil Johnson writes disparagingly 'Is it serious political and social history? Is it perhaps fictionalised history? . . . Or is it really a slice of autobiography, a writer in search of his own past? . . . Certainly the author has no hesitation about thrusting himself into the story . . . the author's cheerful and ebullient ego is there from start to finish, constantly interrupting the historical narrative like an excited commentator bent on shifting attention from the story to the author' (p.19). In the second, Andrew Blake reviews a new journal *Common Knowledge* and says approvingly that its contents demonstrate that 'adding an extra

p-word, personal, to the political, philosophical and psychological does not disable discourse . . . In this overdue re-recognition of the welcome influence of feminist debates about methodology . . . (t)he "I" of the "author" as opposed to and deconstructive of the "we" of the professional "authority" is a most important move towards common knowledge' (p.27).
3. Following Sassoon's (op. cit.) references I read *The Fourth Dimension: Interviews with Christa Wolf* (Wolf 1987), the East German prose writer whose work fuses objective reality, fiction and subjective experience. In these interviews Wolf quotes another writer, Anna Senghers: 'The writer is the curious crossing point where object becomes subject and turns back into object' (1987: 23).
4. Smith argues that women's standpoint is a distinctive one and one from which it is possible to develop new methods and explanations (see Smith 1987, 1988, 1989). The nature of this distinctiveness is to be drawn from women's experiences of oppression and marginalization rather than simply their being women, though Smith has been criticized for not making this clear (see Luxton and Findlay 1989). For explorations of this question of standpoint in terms of race and gender and class see Ladner 1988; Thornton Dill 1988; Etter-Lewis 1991; for gender and disability see Morris 1991. Whilst postmodernism has helped to precipitate an appreciation of standpoints, it has also sometimes done so at the risk of neglecting the social relations of power from which standpoints emerge (see Nicholson 1990; Williams 1992b).
5. To find out about these you generally have to go to literary works, eg. Virginia Woolf's *A Room of One's Own* first published 1929; to biographies, eg. Bair 1990; to interviews, eg. Wolf 1987, op. cit.; or listen to *Desert Island Discs*. Ann Oakley's novel *The Secret Lives of Eleanor Jenkinson* (1992) explores the social, psychological and emotional influences of one woman's development as a writer of fiction.
6. Examples of this are work on 'race', gender and class and social policy (Williams 1987, 1989a, 1993a), learning disability and social policy (Atkinson and Williams 1990; Williams 1989b, 1992a). Recently I've been working on developing frameworks for understanding the relationship between identities, social divisions and welfare needs (Williams 1992b and Williams 1993b).
7. For reasons of space I have not discussed this experience of collaborative writing at the Open University. There is no doubt that the intense and sometimes traumatic give-and-take of constructive criticism that is part of course production has helped crystallize my awareness of what the process of writing is about (discussed later in the chapter).
8. In arguments for the relevance of personal life to the development of knowledge there seems to appear some sort of distinction between what is personal and everyday and what is private. So, for example, Sassoon (op. cit.) seeks to link 'our "private" life outside of our work as professional intellectuals' to 'our professional daily life, that is, some features of the way we work as individuals' (1992: 1). However, Dorothy Smith remarks rather sternly that 'nor . . . am I recommending the self-indulgence of inner exploration or any other enterprise with self as sole focus and object' (1988: 92). It seems to me that one should not distinguish between acceptable and non-acceptable categories of experience, rather concentrate on the methods of allowing the articulation of personal experience to add to our understanding of the social. On the other hand, as Mary Evans (op. cit.) warns, one should beware of telling all and explaining nothing. In any event, whilst telling a personal story, I have played safe and stuck close by my work-life, aware that the drift of the story might not be that different even if it were told through close relationships, deaths of loved ones, sexual identity, or serious illness. For a different personal journey with a neighbouring destination see John Clarke (1991), Chapter 1.

9. Early works we drew on included John Saville's essay '*The welfare state: an historical approach*' written in 1957 (Butterworth and Holman 1975) and Dorothy Wedderburn's *Facts and Theories of the Welfare State* in the 1965 Socialist Register (Wedderburn, 1965).
10. See articles by Hall (1980), and Leonard (1979) in *Marxism Today*.
11. By 'false universalism' here I mean the arguments against the notion of woman as a unitary category advanced by Black feminists like Joseph (1981), Hooks (1982) and Lorde (1984).
12. See Morris (1991).
13. The key political economy of welfare texts were by Gough (1979) and Offe (1984).
14. The term 'essentialism' refers to those explanations of difference (of gender, 'race', disability, etc.) which attribute characteristics to social groups which are deemed to be an essential part of being a member of that group and to mark out the essential difference between that group's members (say, women) and those of its opposite group (men). So, for example, the idea that women by their very nature are caring and that men are, by their very nature, aggressive is an essentialist one. Explanations for these attributes generally reduce them to a single cause – often biological, such as hormonal differences or child-bearing capacities. Such explanations are often associated with traditionalist or reactionary views. For example, the fact that women have children has been used by politicians of the Right to argue for the naturalness of the male breadwinner and nuclear family. But essentialist arguments have also been used by sections of anti-oppressive movements. Some radical feminists have argued for the distinctiveness of women's culture or values, sometimes attributing this to biological difference, sometimes more loosely to a notion of cultural difference (see Williams 1989a).
15. By contrast, social construction theories explain subordination in terms of the way the particular characteristics of oppressed groups are constructed by society. So, for example, it could be argued that it is not women's biology as such which renders women subordinate but the lesser value society places upon child-bearing compared with, say, the development of science and technology. In this situation women, through their relation to child-bearing and all that it involves, are constructed as subordinate (see Sayers 1982).
16. The work of the Centre for Cultural Studies played an important role in making the conceptual vocabulary of Marxism more pliable and accessible. The book *Unpopular Education* was criticised, however, for representing working-class consciousness as rather uniformly ambiguous (Rattansi 1982). For an informative and reflective account of the Centre's work see Clarke 1991, especially for his description of the Centre's attempt to resist the 'individualised and privatized practices which still dominate the mode of academic production' (p.16).
17. It could be argued that these two states of mind represent feminine and masculine sides (speaking symbolically rather than essentialistically). For example, Virginia Woolf talked of the need of the writer to acquire androgyny: 'one must be womanmanly or man-womanly' (1977: 99). Christa Wolf makes a similar suggestion about needing to be both masculine and feminine (1987).
18. For reflective and self-critical accounts of women oral historians crossing the research boundaries of race, class, nationality and culture see the essays in Gluck and Patai (1991), especially those by Hale, Patai and Stacey.

2

Negotiating

Sheila Peace

Unlike other chapters in this book this contribution is not about one piece, or area, of research, rather it reflects upon a career in research in order to try and uncover how the various roles of the researcher, both personal and professional, influence what we know of the research process where, traditionally, the 'self' is kept in the background. These reflections centre on those aspects of the research process which involve negotiation: negotiating with funding bodies; gatekeepers; respondents; obtaining access to settings; deciding who should do what within a research team. It is not concerned directly with the 'negotiation of meanings' in research discussed by other authors in the book (see for example chapters by Dorothy Atkinson, Ann Brechin, Pam Shakespeare and Jan Walmsley).

First then, let us consider negotiation within the context of social research. The Oxford definition of negotiation gives us three options which have validity here:

- confer (with another) with a view to compromise or agreement;
- arrange, bring about (desired result), by negotiating;
- clear, get over or through, dispose of (obstacle, difficulty).

(Concise Oxford Dictionary 1976)

These definitions highlight several issues of importance to this discussion: that relationships are involved; that there is a desired result (for whom?), and that this desired result is obtained through a process which may lead to an agreement, or compromise, or to just getting over the so-called difficulty.

The process of undertaking any piece of social research involves all of these areas, and I shall look at a number of examples below, but first, what else do these definitions imply? To my mind, at the very heart of such negotiations are

expectations about power. It has been said very often that 'social research usually implies the study of the powerless by the powerful' (Wenger 1987: 133). But
one question which arises is just how powerful are the researchers? This question is explored in many of the chapters in this book, but here it forms a central
theme. It begs other questions: If power exists, how does it change within the
context of different relationships? How is this power used? It is here that a
reflection upon one research career may help us to understand more of the
researcher's position of power, or powerlessness, within negotiations.

The personal

To flesh out this researcher we need a biography. Before joining the Open
University in 1990, I had a career in research. Starting as a PhD student pursuing
my own research I then became a research assistant, research officer, international research intern, research fellow, senior research fellow and senior research
officer within the voluntary and academic sectors. I ended this part of my
research career as a senior research officer and founder member of CESSA[1] (Centre for Environmental and Social Studies in Ageing) at the University (then
Polytechnic) of North London. Also during this time, I married and had a child.
     For 12 of these 13 years I worked on contract – shortest two months; longest
three years. Having begun as a geography graduate, I developed an interest and
expertise in gerontology, and in particular in the area of residential care. My
early training was very much on the quantitative side of research methods and
statistical analysis, but a variety of influences, not least my work in applied
social research, the influence of colleagues, anthropologists and sociologists,
and the growing body of work labelled feminist research, led me to develop an
understanding of qualitative research methods and some skills.
     So what does all this information tell us? Stand back and look at it. The basic
material is a white woman with a PhD, one who ages from 25 to 38 years
during this career, who marries and has children, who acquires new skills and
expertise, develops some confidence, goes from working alone to working as
part of a team, but 98 per cent of the time on contract. What power does this
researcher have, this person who on the whole does not feel very powerful?
First, we should make the distinction between having power and feeling
powerful. While I may not feel very powerful, I do recognize that power is
relative and that in different situations I am perceived in different ways.
     Second, we can consider what influences our perceptions of power. There is
the power of organizational status, who you work for, and the respect with
which they are held within a particular field of work. In the case of MIND
(National Federation for Mental Health) and the International Federation on
Ageing, both organizations where I worked in a research capacity, the status of
the organization and what it stood for was a definite plus in negotiations. This
need not have been the case, and I do not think it was in my early days
working at a Polytechnic.
     At a personal level, those aspects of diversity with which we are familiar –
age, sex, class, ethnicity, education – all have a part to play, especially when

it comes to the relationship between status, skills and expertise. For my own part, as for many women, it has been my education, the importance attached to gaining a PhD and the development of expertise which have been powerful tools. I gained expertise by becoming part of a team which managed to maintain a continuity within one field of study, an unusual occurrence for a group of contract research workers. Track records have to be earned and at CESSA, researchers became more influential over time due to specialization, the ability to combine skills, and most importantly personal attributes that meant we enjoyed working together and maintained a 'united front' both to show to the outside world and in support of ourselves. But I realize also that this has been expertise gained at the cost of a working life of some insecurity – both financial and in terms of status. The insecurity of contract research work should not be underplayed for it has immense implications for the power of the researcher. Sitting now in the newly acquired comfort of permanency, such insecurity stills haunts me and keeps me alert to the possibility of further change. I think I am only just learning the value and power of my research experience.

Looking at the personal within a wider context reveals some of the strengths and weaknesses which any individual may bring to negotiations within the research process. We can then ask 'Is there a professional power behind which the individual researcher can hide?' It is to this question that I now turn.

The professional

As an executive member of the Social Research Association during the early 1980s, I witnessed the hard work which went into the development of the set of ethical guide-lines which now underpin membership of the Association. I have often referred to them, especially when teaching students about ethical issues in social research, and turn to them now as a most useful set of clear principles for the professional researcher.

The guide-lines have four sections, each exploring the obligations or responsibilities which researchers have to others:

1 Obligations to society: widening the scope of social research; considering conflicting interests; pursuing objectivity.
2 Obligations to funders and employers: clarifying obligations and roles; assessing alternatives impartially; guarding against pre-empting outcomes; guarding privileged information.
3 Obligations to colleagues: maintaining confidence in research; exposing and reviewing their methods and findings; communicating ethical principles.
4 Obligations to subjects: avoiding undue intrusion; obtaining informed consent (and modifications to informed consent); protecting the interest of subjects; maintaining confidentiality of records; preventing disclosure of identities.

(Social Research Association 1992–3: 78–93)

It is not my intention to review each of these areas here, rather to suggest that they can form the basis for negotiation within the research process which many researchers adopt. They offer guidance on how the professional researcher should behave in relationships with others. But I wonder whether these principles, each laudable in itself, become a mask which you wear as a way of distancing yourself and maintaining your objectivity. Now standing apart from the research process, I wonder whether I have worn this mask for so long that I have internalized the principles without really considering how difficult some of them are to achieve in reality. In the remainder of this chapter I want to explore a variety of situations in which researchers negotiate and look at how a consideration of the personal helps to shed some light on the professional.

Funding bodies and employers

In my potted autobiography I talked about being a contract researcher which may imply that for much of my research career I have been carrying out research which other people have defined. In many cases, a first glance would assume this to be true, but look again and the process of negotiation is at work. The first piece of contract research in which I was engaged was entitled *The Quality of Life of Elderly People in Residential Care: A Feasibility Study of the Development of Survey Measures* (Peace et al. 1979). This research was funded by the Personal Social Services Council (PSSC) but (from where I stood) its conception was really the marrying of two minds, the interests of the PSSC in the subject area and the research group in the methodology. In this case the research group, the Survey Research Unit at the Polytechnic of North London was originated and staffed by former members of the Social Science Research Council (SSRC) Survey Research Unit. They were interested in social indicators of quality of life and their application within welfare settings.

It is the researcher's position in terms of seniority which usually decides whether she or he takes part in 'the talks'. For my part, as the research assistant carrying out the work, I did not negotiate, nor did I question my brief. I got on with it as best I could. Working alone with two supervisors, who were both full-time lecturers, I began as someone who was powerless and very insecure. I had the wrong background in the wrong discipline, but someone had faith in my abilities. My authority increased as I began to be the only person with a complete grasp over the research. It was a combination of youth, gender and inexperience which prevented me from assuming, or being allowed to assume, control over the work.

However, sitting back in the comfort of not having to negotiate does not win research contracts, and in 1981, I was contacted by the Department of Health and Social Security (DHSS Works Division) and asked if colleagues and I would like to tender for a contract to carry out a national consumer study of the residential life of old people in local authority homes. This study was to inform a new edition of the building regulations for Local Authority Residential homes, and the brief focused on the residents' views on their physical environment and how it affected their life satisfaction (Willcocks et al. 1987).

What does this experience tell us about negotiating with funding bodies? First you win the tender and then you negotiate – the funding arrangements; the scale of the study; the methodology; the reporting arrangements and ownership of publications. In this area the SRA guide-lines talk of mutual responsibilities with respect on both sides. They assume 'a common interest which exists between funders or employer and the social researcher as long as the aim of the social inquiry is to advance knowledge' (SRA 1992–3: 81) and that 'social researchers are entitled to expect from a funder or employer respect for the exclusive professional and technical domain and for the integrity of the data' (SRA 1992–3: 82).

In the consumer study of residential life our research team entered negotiations from a very weak position. We were an unknown quantity as far as the funders were concerned. Yet we felt quite strongly that we knew something about the methodology necessary for the study and wanted to exert our influence. Our earlier research had shown how difficult it was to utilize measures of life satisfaction within a structured survey with very old people living in institutional settings (Peace et al. 1981), and we felt that it was crucial that we had some understanding of the process of residential life and the part played by the physical environment in the daily lives of old people. To do this we needed a combination of quantitative and qualitative methods, and negotiations took place over the balance of different types of data.

Negotiations over methods partly reflected the different definitions of the task held by funders and researchers. The funders, represented now by a powerful steering committee, were interested primarily in the fact that this was a national study in a representative sample of homes throughout England – one hundred in all. They were keen on the statistical analysis of data which could be said to be representative. In essence they wanted consumer feedback. We had become more interested in understanding residential life.

So did we get our message across? Were we convincing? I can well remember how 'the ladies from PNL', as one civil servant used to call us, used to quake in their shoes, and my nervous giggle – which is still with me – was very much in evidence (not much power here). In the outcome the study remained a large national survey with a small amount of in-depth qualitative work, and elsewhere we have reported in detail the advantages of even this limited multi-method approach (Kellaher et al. 1990; see also chapter by Moyra Sidell). Through negotiation, the funding body allowed a wide range of material to be collected, but their main interest remained the physical environment, and they required results within 18 months – further work would have to be funded elsewhere (Peace et al. 1986). We had therefore raised the profile of a multi-method approach to data collection and had influenced the agenda but had not changed it.

Negotiation continues throughout the research process, and the national consumer study of residential life also provides us with an example of how policy research can be affected by shifting agendas. Other authors have reported on the hidden agendas which can emerge as research gets underway (McDermott 1987). Both parties can find their interests changing in different ways – the funding body, especially government departments, by social and political change; the researchers by the body of knowledge surrounding the work. I don't think there were any hidden agendas on the part of the funding body at the outset of this research, but we were influenced by political change and as relationships have to be maintained throughout the period of study and beyond, this meant that negotiation became an on-going part of the research.

The major change which altered the course of this research was related to its outcome. As mentioned above the work was commissioned to feed material into new building regulations. However, during the course of the research the government deregulated local authority building works, and as a result, the building note was no longer required.[2] So we were left with material for a building note that was not going to be made mandatory. The negotiations started again, this time over funding for a different way of disseminating the material. In the end the DHSS put up a small amount of money to pay us to write what we saw as an alternative building note; *A Balanced Life* (Peace et al. 1982), which it was left to us to disseminate as best we could.

These experiences, during the course of one project, tell us a number of things about negotiations with funding bodies and the expected role of the researcher. When the subject to be researched originates with the funding body, as in government-funded research, then the researchers never really hold the balance of power, although they can find ways to influence the research process and its outcome (Hadley 1987; Booth 1988; Pahl 1992). It is expertise which is valued on the researcher's side. If you have a 'good track record' that will help; if you have had a grant from them before, completed on time, came up with something they can use and have published widely, then you stand even more chance of being funded again. If the idea is yours and you send your proposal to the Economic and Social Research Council (ESRC) or another major funding body, then peer review comes into play and many of the same unwritten rules outlined above apply. Hitting the right project at the right time, when your subject area is seen as fashionable in terms of policy-making always helps. As a professional researcher this means playing by the rules, being efficient, competent, reliable and not too radical. As an individual I know that this means hard work, sleepless nights and the value of team-work.

Access to – and within – research settings

Much of the research with which I have been involved has meant negotiating access to both settings and people. Here the question of who you are and who you represent is often crucial. If funded by a government department then the fact that you are working on their behalf may seem to add weight to your case, but this is not always so. Central government policy is obviously perceived in different ways at a local level, and clarification over the aims and objectives of the study may be sought at length. It is here that different interpretations of the research may make a subtle difference as to who does and who does not take part. The researchers will state that they will do their best to 'tell it as it really is' and remain objective, but respondents will be influenced by the overall objectives of the project, as well as what they know of the researchers' work and the institution they represent. In these situations researchers may find their own institutional base more useful in allowing them to negotiate access.

However, to help them with their negotiations researchers can enlist the help of other powerful groups. In the research carried out at CESSA throughout the 1980s we developed a particular style of working. We made sure that we informed the research committee of the Association of Directors of Social Services (ADSS) of our proposed research, indeed we sought their approval. Working within the area of residential care and its regulation, this type of support made sense. We wanted to carry people with us and not alienate them. Our research projects have all had steering committees. While we may have found the committee for the consumer study of residential life daunting, we learnt that it was influential, could be very critical, but also could be very supportive. We felt we needed this. In a later study of the development of the regulatory framework for residential care funded by the Joseph Rowntree Memorial Trust, we carried out field work in eight local authority social services departments, going back repeatedly over an eighteen month period (Kellaher et al. 1988). We also carried out two national postal surveys within social services' departments. The negotiations for this level of involvement with local government were facilitated by the members of the Association of Metropolitan Authorities and Association of County Councils who sat on the steering committee for this project.

In the end negotiations over access have to come down to face-to-face discussions, although there is often a long way to go before this encounter is reached. Sometimes this process seems endless. When the access is to a residential home, discussions will seldom be with the Director of Social Services, but there is a hierarchy of approval which must be sought, and woe betide you if you miss a level. At this point I should add that when working with the private care sector, although direct negotiation has to be made with individual homes, the approval of the professional associations for home owners always proved beneficial – again another powerful group. So, negotiations are carried out through letters, phone calls and meetings, and all the time you have to state your case, explain what it is you are trying to do, be nice to people and hope that they feel that the project is worth their time and effort.

Gatekeepers and respondents

In the following chapter Jan Walmsley looks in more detail at explaining research, especially to gatekeepers and respondents. Here I shall touch briefly on my own experience, bearing in mind the theme of negotiating and positions of power. Working within residential settings the main gatekeeper to setting, staff and residents is the head of home; in the private sector, proprietor/manager (who may or may not be the same person). The first meeting with the head of home is crucial. His or her knowledge of your project will have been gathered from written information and telephone conversations.

The written information will often contain a long statement of the research objectives and methods; the telephone conversation will, no doubt, have been brief, with explanations modified sometimes out of all recognition from the original. You say you will explain in detail when you meet.

As part of the negotiation over access, your explanation of the research is particularly important. At the end of it you would like to think that the person had some idea of what was expected, how much time it would take, how it would disrupt their routines, etc. In this situation it is the head of home who has the power to refuse access or to set limits on your plans. If the research is to involve both interviews and observations, as much of our work has done, then residents and staff in the home are being asked to put up with the disruption of a stranger, or strangers, in their midst. The task then is to negotiate access whilst remembering those obligations set out in the SRA guide-lines – 'avoid undue intrusion', 'obtain informed consent', 'protecting the interest of the subjects'. In my case I think these occasions offer some of the most explicit examples of the personal and professional mix. During negotiations with heads of home, staff or older people, I always seemed to find myself drawing upon some experience or other. In my case, I have worked as both a ward orderly in a large hospital and as a domestic and care assistant in residential homes while a student. On reflection one of my favourite stories was about scrubbing the white tiles in the hallway of the home with bleach until they gleamed – Matron was very keen on gleam. This was 1972.

I had versions of this story depending on whom I was talking to, stories which helped me convey that I did know a bit about residential life, I wasn't a complete novice. But what was I trying to do? Was I trying to put them at their ease and, in the case of the head of home or the care staff, also show that I could be helpful and so 'avoid undue intrusion'? Was I divesting myself of my professional mask by showing that I could be 'just one of the workers', or was I adding to my power by showing that I was a researcher, but I could also do their job, or did I just want to be liked? Elsewhere in this book Pam Shakespeare and Dorothy Atkinson discuss similar experiences concerning the researcher's role.

With the older people I am conscious now, although probably unconscious then through sheer nerves, that I also had a story to tell. This time it was about my grandparents, the residents I had helped to look after, or a lady called Mrs Eaton and her friend Kate, whom I used to visit on a regular basis as a Community Service Volunteer (Kate was always called Kate out of preference, whereas Mrs Eaton was never called Mildred). During the years I visited them Kate had moved into a residential home, and I took Mrs Eaton to see her there. She hated the trips but felt we must go. I know now that I used these experiences to help me relate to the experiences of residents, and in so doing I negotiated the interviews. While residents potentially had the power to say 'no' to my requests, in most cases as a captive audience few dared to refuse (see Booth 1983, 1993 forthcoming). I hoped my stories had the effect of putting them at their ease so that they would feel comfortable answering my questions.

With the 1000 older people interviewed in the consumer study of residential life we took a stratified sample from each home. Each chosen person was given written information about the project which stated that it was being done for the DHSS, and if they agreed to take part, they were asked to sign a consent form. In some cases relatives signed the form for them. This was not ideal but with 100 homes and 1000 residents, seemed the only feasible process at the time.

In a more recent study, CESSA has been undertaking action research whereby residents are involved as equal participants within a process of quality assurance in residential homes (CESSA 1992). Here, a group of people, including residents, from inside and outside the home, undertake to talk to all residents and staff about life in the home. However, no-one is compelled or obliged to take part. We have come some way then from negotiations with residents that are totally one-sided, to those where some older people are becoming active participants within the research process. In handing over the tools of research, you also hand over the responsibilities, and in residential settings particular issues such as confidentiality need to be considered carefully. You can see why it is easier for a researcher to come in from outside and assume these responsibilities, but it is wrong to think that only researchers can carry out these roles. The balance of power within negotiations is shifting in favour of those formerly powerless, but there is still a long way to go.

One further aspect of negotiations which these developments highlight is the nature of research relationships in terms of reciprocity. In a way research must often seem to the respondent as a very one-sided process. What exactly do you have to offer as a researcher? The advancement of knowledge seems very abstract and within applied social research very inadequate. Data gathered in any one residential home could be used for training purposes; for looking at care planning; for re-evaluating the underlying principles of the home. But when staff and residents are asked to take part in a national study related to the design of future provision, or to try out a research method in order to see how it works, then participation can become an act of faith. Greater involvement in the research process should ensure that all participants feel that they own part of the outcome.

The research team

Of course negotiations are not only confined to those encounters with funders, steering committees and the subjects of research; negotiations also go on between researchers. In the SRA guide-lines, 'obligations to colleagues', which may lead to negotiations, are voiced in terms of the wider research community and point to aspects of professional practice. The experiences of negotiating between colleagues which I had in mind are more parochial, and differ depending on whether you are working alone with supervisors, or as part of a research team. I want to talk here mainly about the experience of teams. In any piece of research, the personal and professional lives of the researchers can affect the outcome. In multi-disciplinary teams it may be obvious who is going to do what within the group, but this is not always the case, and key questions can arise over seniority, experience and skill, especially when it comes to who is going to be doing the bulk of the fieldwork, and who owns the research, those who had the ideas or those who did the leg work. Again, these are all examples of power relationships between team members and in my experience can often be linked to differences of discipline and method, (for example those with statistical skills versus those without, those seen as quantitative researchers versus those seen as qualitative), gender differences and expectations over career development, which can be particularly fraught in the contract research world. Of course these areas are often all intimately interrelated.

So, the professional can become personal and vice versa. One further example demonstrates this quite clearly. During the study of regulation mentioned above, I became pregnant with my first child, and one of my colleagues got another job within the Polytechnic. The team therefore had to do a lot of re-shuffling, two colleagues (one senior, one junior) ended up carrying the fieldwork, which involved long periods away from home. I was grounded to the office analysing a national postal survey. After four months maternity leave,[3] I returned to the project with my new time constraints. We soldiered on and completed the study. We didn't really negotiate these changes, the group was too small and did not have spare capacity. As we were working on contract, change just had to be accommodated, and I know that this placed an enormous strain on some members of the team. But I also think that part of the lack of negotiation came because we were all friends as well as colleagues; we didn't want to let each other down or our collective (and individual) reputation(s) down. But some of us ended up feeling guilty and others overstretched. The outcome had both positive and negative consequences – some gained responsibility which they wouldn't normally have assumed; others lost it or re-channelled it elsewhere. It was experience to be used as members of the team developed their careers in other directions.

Conclusions – negotiations throughout the research process

I suppose that it is common to think that most of the negotiating within research goes on in the early stages, that once you have agreed the aims and objectives, and have gained access to your subject then you are home and dry. But, as this chapter has shown, research is an on-going process of negotiating. In a two- or three-year study you always have to be open to change and renegotiation. What happens when things do not work out as planned, or when you cannot get access to respondents or settings you wished to study? Over the years I can think of a range of experiences where 'spanners were thrown in the works': response rates in postal questionnaires which proved disappointing even after intense telephone reminders; access to settings that were denied due to misunderstandings, caution, overwork; respondents who backed out at the last minute and could not be persuaded to change their minds; material that arrived too late to be included; statistical analysis in which, upon reflection, we had little confidence, even though the statistical test said otherwise. At all these points we had to stand back and re-negotiate – our time, our resources, the aims and objective of the study and, most important of all, our obligations to others.

I return then to the fact that negotiations within the research process are about relationships. Relationships that may be between parties with vested interests, hidden agendas and unequal power. The self-negotiation which individuals undertake when they embark on a piece of research is to define their own position within the bounds of professional practice. How far 'the self' is allowed to intrude upon the research process, and how far it should, is still open to debate. We have seen in this chapter that during negotiations the position of the researcher can vary depending on the circumstances, and the power or powerlessness of all those involved.

Acknowledgements

I would like to thank Leonie Kellaher, Director of CESSA for her helpful comments on a second draft of this chapter.

Notes

1. The author remains a Research Associate at CESSA.
2. It is interesting to note here that at this time, private residential care homes were beginning to develop, and the subsequent regulatory framework (Registered Homes Act 1984; Residential Care Homes Regulations 1984, and the code of practice Home Life) involving registration and inspection still refers new proprietors to the last building note in 1973 (DHSS and Welsh Office 1973). The fact that our research recommended standards for the physical environment in advance of this building note was later indicated in a government circular (DHSS 1986).
3. As a contract researcher maternity leave was not part of my terms and conditions of employment, and after much negotiation was finally paid for by the Polytechnic and CESSA itself.

3

Explaining

Jan Walmsley

Explaining to ourselves – explaining to others

I: What do you want to tape it for. For the college or what?

J: I'd better tell you a bit more about myself, hadn't I? I suppose, well, I'm at the Open University, have you heard of that?

I: No.

J: No, well it's in Milton Keynes and I'm doing a sort of student project if you like. It's called research.

I: Yeh.

J: And what I'm doing is trying to find out about people who've been in hospital or go to ATCs (Adult Training Centres) or whatever but who are also helping other people.

I: Yeh.

J: In ways that some people get paid for if you see what I mean.

I: Yeh.

(Research interview transcript 1991)

Research is rather an esoteric activity: as McCall and Simmons put it (1969) 'What motives, what alien causes, would lead a man (sic) to turn on his brethren with an analytic eye.' What indeed. We may be hard put to explain to ourselves; how can we explain to others?

In this excerpt above, taken from the first of 42 interviews I have undertaken as the fieldwork for a postgraduate degree, I am fumbling to explain, honestly, what I am about. It is not, looking back, a very adequate explanation. You, the reader, are as much in the dark as was Isobel on that occasion. Do you understand what Isobel is being asked to do? Do you want to know more? Perhaps you can empathize with my struggle to explain myself, to find common ground and shared experiences to build on. The extract illustrates the point made by Lazarsfeld, that the shared contexts and assumptions of daily question and answer are absent from the interview situation (cited in Mishler 1986: 1).

This chapter focuses on the explanations we give about our research to the people we are researching, and considers the implications of those explanations for the research. It argues that explanations are important, perhaps central, to research, yet are intensely problematic. It also addresses the question of how we explain to ourselves why we are doing research at all.

This chapter has some themes in common with others in the book, particularly its immediate predecessor, 'Negotiating'. In her chapter, Sheila Peace writes from the perspective of a contract researcher for whom one explanation, at least, is obvious; it is a means to earn a living. I write as a 'mature' part-time postgraduate student for whom such an explanation is unconvincing, both to myself and to others. In a different sense there are overlaps with Dorothy Atkinson's 'Relating' and Ann Brechin's 'Sharing'; we are all undertaking research with people with learning difficulties,[1] and draw on that research for our chapters. How far issues raised in research with people with learning difficulties translate to other social groups is something to be considered; I return to this at the end of the chapter.

My interest in how research is explained was stimulated by the work of William Foot Whyte (1955). In undertaking qualitative research the researcher aims to penetrate different worlds, to understand people's perceptions of their world, and to explain those perceptions. And s/he becomes, for a time, part of their world. The Methodological Appendix to Foot Whyte's 'Street Corner Society', describes how he gained access to Cornerville, his research setting. After some unpromising failures, such as trying to pick up a woman and being offered a fast transit down the nearest staircase, he was introduced to Doc, a resident of Cornerville. He explained his project to Doc, whose reply was:

> any nights you want to see anything I'll take you around. I can take you to the joints . . . gambling joints . . . I can take you around to the street corners. Just remember that you're my friend. That's all they need to know.
>
> (Foot Whyte 1955: 85)

Doc was right. Tagging along with Doc gave Foot Whyte the access he needed. But later on, as he moved around without Doc, explanations were required:

> as I was hanging about Cornerville I found I needed an explanation for my study – I began with rather an elaborate explanation. I was studying the social history of Cornerville . . . but I had a new angle – I was quite pleased with the explanation at the time, but no one else seemed to care for it. I gave the explanation on only two occasions and each time when I had finished there was an awkward silence – it was apparently too involved to mean anything to Cornerville people – I soon found people were developing their own explanations about me: I was writing a book about Corner-

ville. This might seem too vague as an explanation yet it sufficed. I found
that my acceptance in the district depended on the personal relationships
I developed far more than any explanation I might give. If I was alright
then my project was alright; if I was no good, then no amount of explanation could convince them that the book was a good idea.

(Foot Whyte 1955: 89)

This anecdote highlights some important areas. Whyte regarded the relationships he developed as more important than explanations. But he spent three
years in Cornerville. He lived there. Many of us have less time and freedom but
still claim to do research, and must to some extent rely on explanations of
what we are doing.

Implicit in Whyte's account is the assumption that research is not an everyday feature of the lives of the people he went to study. Lofland and Lofland
(1984) suggest that even when people know they are being studied they probably have only a tenuous idea about what the researcher is doing, and why.

In order to gain access to research participants, the researcher develops a set of
explanations about what he or she is doing. I explore explanations, and their
significance, with reference to two projects I have undertaken as a part-time
postgraduate student based at the Open University. Both projects involved semi-
structured interviews with people with learning difficulties. The first entailed
interviews with five people at an Adult Training Centre (MSc dissertation), and
sought to ascertain what meaning they attributed to the term 'adulthood'. The
second, a doctoral thesis, included forty-two interviews with 22 people about
their experiences of giving and receiving care. For the sake of brevity, I will refer
to the first project as *Adulthood*, and the second as *Caring*.

Explaining: getting into the field

This is the first step into the world of the research participants. I do not work
directly with people with learning difficulties and have to rely on others. I am
fortunate enough to have been involved for some years in producing and
disseminating courses in the learning difficulties field which are highly regarded and widely used. This has given me more than a passing acquaintance
with local service providers, tutors and managers who, if their interest can be
engaged, offer access to people in my research population.

For the caring project I set out to interview a variety of people. It was not
enough to locate a captive population in an Adult Training Centre (ATC),
school or hospital. I wanted to locate people who had at some time in their
lives been labelled as having learning difficulties, including people who had
escaped the traditional 'career' followed by the majority – special school, Adult
Training Centre, and/or residential care. This certainly served to complicate
access.

One example illustrates this complexity. Gaining access to one participant,
Eileen, involved a whole series of explanations. Beginning with Jeannie, a
Special Needs tutor I knew through my work, I was passed to her colleague,

Helen. Helen could not help personally, but gave me the name of the local MENCAP organizer, Ruth. When I phoned Ruth, Helen had already done some explaining for me. I felt anxious as I dialled, having put it off for many specious reasons for some time, but it became clear that Ruth had been forewarned and had a list of six people who more or less fell into the category I was looking to interview. She gave me the names. Then it was a matter of asking how to contact them. For one woman, Eileen, I was referred to the Adult Training Centre. More explanations, first to the ATC receptionist, then to Karen, Eileen's key worker, finally to Eileen herself on the phone. Eileen agreed to see me. Back to Karen, the key worker – had I got permission? No, I had not spoken to the ATC manager, nor Eileen's family. The ATC manager was on holiday for two weeks. Karen offered to explain to the Deputy Manager, and to Eileen's family. She rang me back later that day. Much to my relief the answer was yes – but Karen reported that Eileen's sister had said I wouldn't be asking anything personal would I . . . ?

What do we learn from this? The explanations are multiple – in Eileen's case the explanation was made to at least eight people – the layers of communication are complex, the possibilities for misunderstandings are huge, it all felt precarious. If the receptionist had not been helpful, if Karen had been more suspicious, if the Deputy Manager, etc, etc. What it tells us about the status of Eileen, an adult woman, is that she is surrounded by people, all of whom, it seems, could veto her participation. I became subject to some of the constraints to which Eileen is subject. I felt I could barely move without asking the permission of numerous people. It gave me an insight into how 'caring' operated as benevolent control for Eileen. I was left wondering if there was not an easier way . . . and perhaps if the explanation had been better . . .

Explaining the research: for colleagues and intermediaries

In order to explain one's purpose to gatekeepers, intermediaries and participants, one finds oneself translating the research into a new language. To gain credibility in my academic peer group it had been necessary to frame the research in a particular way, using words such as, 'care', 'life histories', 'ethnography'. These are not necessarily words which mean anything to people outside the ivory tower. For the intermediaries it was still necessary to think myself into their frame of reference to abbreviate, to simplify. It was a time of testing. Would people understand? Would they want to help? I was lucky. I struck a vein of enthusiasm, and found an echoing chord. The project meant something to others. The responses to my explanations fed both into the research itself and into my next set of explanations, to research participants.

Explaining the research: for research participants

My research is with people who are of interest because of an ascribed characteristic: learning difficulties. I am interested in speaking to them because they have this label. It's my reason for using intermediaries, to locate such people. The first, and to my mind, the biggest problem is negotiating this minefield. If I explained outright that I was interested in people because they belong to a stigmatized group, I was taking a risk. I had no idea whether they accepted the label as part of their identity, or whether they would be resistant and angry at the suggestion. The approach through intermediaries only partially avoided the problem. I could glide over it because people were known to the service as belonging to that group. But could I assume they know that, and that that is why I was there. It was this I was skirting round with Isobel (see the beginning of this chapter). I did not want to confront her with the term 'learning difficulties'.

This issue cropped up continually. On one occasion I asked one of the intermediaries for the names of women with learning difficulties who have children. No one in my initial sample fell into this category. After several weeks she rang up in great excitement. She had the names of four women with children and had negotiated for me to meet them. Each one had to be approached individually. Two wanted to meet me with a tutor present, at least initially. The other two were on the phone and I was to ring them to arrange a time and place to meet. I duly rang one of these, Sheila, a woman with five children living with her husband in a nearby town. We agreed to meet the following week. On the phone I did not attempt to explain my research. There were noisy children in the background, and Sheila said she was about to go out. The day came for our interview and I set off. I found myself in a pleasant council estate, partly owner occupied. Sheila had been waiting for me. She stepped out to welcome me, and had a pot of tea ready. Was this a woman with learning difficulties? She challenged all my stereotypes. My first question to her when we sat down, contrary to my normal practice (to discuss the weather, and generally make small talk), was to ask her if she regarded herself as someone with learning difficulties. She immediately said she did, and I relaxed. Had she rejected the label, I am not sure what I could have done. Pam Shakespeare's chapter explores how the researcher feels constrained by the rules of polite conversation, and this example is a nice illustration of the dilemma she describes. My role as researcher, wanting to make sure I had the right sort of person, conflicted with my role as a person, wanting to avoid making the informant feel embarrassed.

Explaining the questions

In principle I see it as an ethical litmus test of the research question, if it can be explained to the research population without too many uncomfortable euphemisms. How can you justify asking people to reveal details of their lives without telling them what you are trying to find out? Sheila Peace explores this in her chapter 'Negotiating'. In explaining my caring research, I tried to be quite honest, but, there were problems.

One of these was the use of language. The people with learning difficulties I interviewed did not, on the whole, use the word 'care', a term understood by academics and by service providers, but not necessarily by service users. I do not think participants always understood what I meant when I said I wanted to know about their experiences of care. After a number of interviews I translated this into 'helping' or 'looking after' because most people did use these words. In effect, the research itself fed the explanations.

Sometimes explanations can work only too well. Eileen knew that I wanted to interview her because she cares for her elderly father. This seems to have actually framed her identity for me, to the extent that when she was introducing herself to a group at a conference she said: 'My name is Eileen; I look after my dad'. I have an uneasy feeling that this was for my benefit, to prove she was the person I had hoped to find as an interviewee. In addition, as Whyte found, people with learning difficulties do not necessarily appreciate what research is, or why anyone might want to do it. Concrete explanations appear to work better: Whyte said he was writing a book. I told Isobel I was 'doing a sort of student project'.

Looking back on my earlier Adulthood project I find I was vague in explaining my research. The research is entitled 'The meaning of adulthood in the lives of some people with learning difficulties'. Yet I did not explain that, at least not at first. How could I? It felt insulting to imply people's adulthood was questionable, or to suggest that they had learning difficulties, even though they were clients of an ATC. Yet not being able to clearly explain the purpose of my research may well have mystified people, and they may have given answers to the wrong question!

Explaining yourself as researcher

The further I moved from the familiar academic world where I began, the more problematic it became to explain myself and my role. Not only did I need to enter the world of the research population, I needed to explain parts of my world to them. At times I began to doubt the motives which brought me to them. It is tempting to gloss over this, especially in learning difficulties research. The researcher moves in and does not explain who she is, and why she is there. Yet people are unlikely just to accept that we are researchers and leave it at that. They will seek to make sense of our activities by slotting us into their frames of reference. Sylvia Bercovici undertook some research with people with learning difficulties. She comments:

> It took many months to convince 'natives' of this system that the researcher was not part of the collaborative network they saw as an immutable part of life – they had no social type in their classification system that corresponded to the identity the research wanted them to perceive and understand.
>
> (1981: 139)

In working with people with learning difficulties we are perhaps faced most starkly with the issue of how the researcher is perceived. In lives which are frequently the subject of surveillance or assessment of one kind or another it must be quite hard to understand the researcher who comes in purporting to be – what? A disinterested observer? A friend or ally? A seeker after knowledge? Dorothy Atkinson quotes some insights into this in describing her research interviews:

> *Alice Wise to her social worker:* She's very nice isn't she. I thought she'd be strict and horrible.
>
> *Joyce Hardcastle:* Are you an important social services person? Are you very high up? Edgar said you were.
>
> *Edward Hayes to his social worker:* She must be very important asking us all these questions.
>
> (Atkinson 1988: 69)

We should not be surprised that people seek to make sense of what we are doing. Most social interaction is predicated upon our understanding of who we are addressing. Usually we are embarrassed if the person to whom we are talking turns out to be another customer, if we think we are addressing a shop assistant. Indeed, people who cannot modulate their responses to the person with whom they are interacting are often labelled as socially inadequate. Yet how we explain our research to the people we are researching is something that's little discussed in research reports – as is how we in our turn have been perceived.

I suspect that people with learning difficulties are likely to slot the researcher into the panoply of professionals whose business it is to find out about their lives, unless and until alternative explanations become more plausible. One of the people I interviewed, Louise, was keen to tell me how unhappy she was living with her father. From this I obtained many insights into her relationship with him. But I feel sure she told me this partly because she believed I could help to find her alternative accommodation. At no point did I imply this. But just by being me, apparently important enough to be an interviewer, she obtained that impression. I gained – but at the expense of an unwitting deception. The sad thing is, you may never know how people explained you to themselves, yet that might be crucially important.

Avoiding explanations

There is a tendency, often irresistible, to fudge explanations. To illustrate this I use an excerpt from my first Adulthood project interview:

> the reason I've asked to meet you is to talk to you about your self-advocacy group which has been going for at least three years I think . . . I'm a student you see and I have to do some work which involves talking to people about their lives and how they manage them. Now why I really wanted to meet you was to talk about the group . . .
>
> (Walmsley 1988)

I said nothing about adulthood, nothing about having learning difficulties.

Already I had begun to hide my real intentions, and to take on an identity, that of student, which I imagined would have some meaning. I was, in what I then thought was a polite and respectful way, avoiding any awkward issues. Not surprisingly, no one responded to my invitation to ask questions.

In the subsequent one-to-one interviews I also tried to explain my role, or at least I did after the first one which, when I looked back at the transcript, appeared to have begun with a discussion about how full the post-boxes are at Christmas! With Sarah I had little success:

> *J:* Right, so I was hoping if you don't mind telling me about your group home, your move, and what you are hoping from it. But I must explain first that I don't have any influence over what happens to you, right, just curiosity. Don't worry. Whatever you say I am not going to tell Bob [social worker], what you say is just between us. I'm not a spy or anything, OK? 'Cos I think people often wonder why people like me are doing what we are doing, but I'm not doing anything that's going to change things for you. Is that OK?
>
> *S:* Yes.
>
> *J:* Is there anything you want to ask me before you start? Any questions?
>
> *S:* I had a little bother. Two boys, they keep ringing me up.

Looking back this seems quite defensive, almost as if I had no explanation worthy of the name. What could Sarah have said? Clearly I hadn't tuned in to Sarah's agenda, and was too preoccupied with my own ethical hang-ups.

Colin was quite different.

> *J:* First thing I must say is I haven't any official connection with this place so whatever you say will be between us. Do you want to ask me anything?
>
> *C:* Um what does your course that you're doing at the Open University offer you?

Later, right at the end of the interview he came back to the question:

> *J:* Is there anything else you want to say before we finish?
>
> *C:* Um what do you get at the end of your course?

I answered at some length, and I remember feeling pleased and relieved that at least one of the people had taken my explanation on, and felt able to question me about my side of the story. It made for a semblance of reciprocity. It is interesting, though, that he chose to focus on the one concrete thing I had said, that I was a student. Perhaps I was right in thinking that was a meaningful identity. But perhaps I was mistaken in not being more up front about my project, or in not having a project I felt I could explain directly.

After all this, does it matter? Does it matter whether people thought I was a member of staff or a social worker or a student? Does it matter whether participants understand what the researcher is about, or indeed what research is? The answer depends on whether you are willing to see research subjects as passive data sources or as active adults who seek to make sense of the situations they are in, and whether you believe that there is an objective truth that can be arrived at through finding the perfect method, the perfect interviewer, the perfect hermeneutical data analysis.

As you may have guessed, I believe that people do try to make sense of situations, and that there is no final truth; the explanations you make, and the perceptions people have of you, the researcher, all feed into the data, and alter it. It is therefore important to take explanations seriously, and to reflect on how people explain you to themselves. Dean and Foot Whyte (1978) argue that asking whether the informant is telling the truth is irrelevant. What is important is understanding why they present themselves as they do. Their view of the researcher will have a crucial bearing on what they say, and how they say it.

Franco Ferrarotti puts it more strongly:

> The observer is radically implicated in his research, that is in the field of the object under investigation. The latter, far from being passive, continually modifies his behaviour according to the behaviour of the observer. This circular feedback process renders any presumption of objective knowledge simply ridiculous.
>
> (1981: 20)

Explaining is an interactive process. In trying to explain yourself and your research to the participants you are taking a step into their world. From the reactions you get, from the feedback, you adjust your explanations, and you adjust your perception of their world. That moves you on just a shade each time – if you allow it to.

In the Adulthood project I think my unease about my explanations, or lack of them, was heightened by the very subject I was researching – adulthood. In retrospect, I felt that by not telling people much about the research, I was not treating them as adults. I addressed this in the 'Reflexive account' in the research report:

> the emphasis in my original research proposal on adulthood was helpful in a fundamental way. It alerted me to the importance of choosing a method which accorded respect to people . . . because the research aims were not concrete, I avoided detailed explanations about what I was trying to achieve. I tried to ensure they had a certain freedom of action, but it was unclear whether this was a real or a token freedom.
>
> (Walmsley 1989: 42)

It was a pilot project. It taught me a hard lesson: that next time I must find a research project that could be explained.

Feelings generated by the process of explaining

I have found the whole process of explaining quite uncomfortable. Part of the anxiety was letting go, relying on the understanding and integrity of the intermediaries. Would they select people with the right characteristics, or would they find people who they knew would be co-operative, polite and say nice things. Would they forget that I wanted to speak to people in a particular category, and present me with someone who was older or younger than my carefully constructed sampling frame required? If so, how did I say no? Or did I say yes, and change once more the carefully constructed sampling frame? (Usually I did the latter.)

I had given someone else the job of explaining me and my research. How would they do it? Would I ever know? I felt I had lost control when I left it to Eileen's key worker to negotiate for me. Luckily it was OK, but it need not have been. How could I undo other people's explanations, if they weren't what I had intended? I also felt I was asking for favours. What could I offer in return? I felt I had little to offer. Perhaps, most importantly, I was aware of perpetrating deceptions by not explaining fully the implications of taking part in the research. Did people understand they would become one of a sample, have their words dissected, examined and put together again to make some abstractions? Yet, I knew I lacked the skills to explain that.

These reflections are rather negative – that the research is frustrating, uncomfortable, an abuse of power – maybe a waste of time. This leads into a discussion of why it's done at all; how do you explain that to yourself?

Explaining your research to yourself

So finally, to return to the first and last person to whom the research must be explained, oneself. Much of the discomfort expressed in this chapter stems from the fact that, like much research, the research I undertake has no obvious functional outcome. I cannot convince myself that, once I have completed it, life will be better for those many people who have helped me on the way, that they will necessarily understand themselves better, or increase their income, or self esteem, or whatever. The benefits will not be concrete and tangible. If it is only a means to the end of furthering my own career that is, for me, insufficient justification.

But I know it is more than that; the outcomes may be intangible, and infinitesimal when compared to the output of the whole knowledge industry, but there will, I believe, be benefits. One of these is that I am struggling to find ways of hearing the voices of people with learning difficulties. I am making many mistakes. It could be done better. But by writing about the process honestly, I hope I can help others build on my work, so that those voices can be heard more clearly, more loudly in future. There has been so much injustice done that we need to know about it so that we can fight against it. This was not part of the explanations I gave people. At the outset it seemed too ambitious. It is only now, on reflection, that I believe it.

Second, I intend that what I discover will eventually be communicated to people with learning difficulties so that they can begin to understand the social and historical processes which have led to stigma and segregation. Self advocacy is now recognized and relatively well established. The next step is to reclaim the past as women have done, as gay men and lesbians, and black people are doing. 'We need the past in order to be able to understand ourselves. We need it in order to believe in our future. If we have come from nowhere where are we going to?' (Hall Carpenter Archives 1989: 1).

The need for a past applies as much to people with learning difficulties as to other social groups. If my research makes a small contribution to reconstructing that past through the words of people who have lived it, that will be sufficient explanation for doing it. In this chapter I have dwelt on the way research is explained to the people who are being researched. I have meditated on the significance of the explanation in determining the research data we gather. It is in some ways quite a narrow focus. I hope I have demonstrated its importance.

Explaining is central to the research process. How far do the issues raised here apply to groups other than people with learning difficulties? The answer is a tentative one, as my experience is limited. Certainly, negotiation with multiple gatekeepers is most likely when adults are in some kind of institutional care. Those of my respondents who live in their own homes and have telephones have been able to answer for themselves when approached. Therefore the determining factor for access is not respondents having learning difficulties as such, but their social situation. I would suggest, however, that the need to think oneself into another person's frame of reference is crucial in any research of this kind; it is perhaps most obvious when the research is with people who are markedly different from the researcher in terms of social and cultural factors, but is equally important to be aware of possibilities for misunderstandings when this is not the case. Rene, a person I interviewed as a parent of a man with learning difficulties, said to me on my second visit 'now I have a clear idea of what you are doing I can answer your questions more helpfully'. But I'd written her a detailed explanation, and spoken to her twice on the phone – I'd thought we understood one another at the outset. I discovered that it took more than letters and initial phone calls to establish understanding.

In all research situations, how we explain our research, and how the people being researched explain it to themselves is a subject worthy of attention, more attention than is usually given to it. It can be a crucial determinant of what we discover.

Note

1. The term 'people with learning difficulties' is used here to describe people who have been labelled at some point in their lives as requiring specialist mental handicap services. 'People with learning difficulties' is the label preferred by People First, an umbrella organization which speaks for people formerly labelled as 'people with mental handicap', and I have followed their lead in adopting the term.

4

Observing

Alyson Peberdy

At the beginning of the 1980s I spent two years in a New Guinea village as a participant observer both observing and, to some extent, joining in a way of life with which I was very unfamiliar. This chapter is a reflection on some of the things I learnt about the process of observing people and social relationships during that period.

Observation is in some ways rather like breathing: life depends on it and we do it all the time, usually without reflection. The observational skills of watching, listening, counting and identifying patterns of social interaction are processes we tend to take for granted though we would, quite literally, be lost without them. Watching how to catch the attention of the waiter in a busy restaurant or trying to discover a seating arrangement that leads to fewer family arguments at the dinner table are just two illustrations of the kind of familiar activity that involves highly developed observational skills.

In everyday life it is usually only when things do not work out in some way that it becomes necessary to consciously reflect on such skills and the way in which we use them in our relationships with other people. This happens when others observe our observation and experience it as impolite, intrusive or even threatening. It also happens when we do not achieve the goal we were intending. Failing to catch the eye of the waiter in the busy restaurant, we may decide to become more observant, watching not only the position of the tables but noticing also the clothing and accents of the most successful customers. Sometimes we have to acknowledge that the goal, rather than the method of observation, needs to be modified. Perhaps family arguments at the dinner table occur whatever the seating arrangement.

My own experience of observation in social research follows a similar pattern. In the normal run of things I have got on with it in a largely unquestioning way until I've been made to stop and think. Perhaps someone has objected to what I have been doing, or I just felt things weren't working out. It is at these points I have had to think in depth about the nature and role of observation and to question the assumptions and values underlying my observational activities.

Junker (1960) has usefully distinguished four roles social researchers may adopt in relation to a group or community they are observing. At one end of the spectrum is the intensely involved role of *complete participant* who acts as a full and ordinary member of the group being studied, by, for example, actually joining a religious sect (see, for instance, Jules-Rosette 1975). At the opposite end is the *complete observer* who has no contact at all with those being observed (as when watching a group through a one-way mirror). Between the two lies *participant as observer* and *observer as participant* (depending on the degree of involvement with the people being studied). As a general rule observation that involves a high degree of involvement tends to be especially useful when there are important differences between the views of outsiders and insiders (as with a religious sect or ethnic group) or when the phenomenon is hidden from public view (for instance drug users and dealers).

It is important to notice that in Junker's model participation and observation tend to be seen as competing and conflicting objectives: accuracy and reliability are best achieved by minimizing participation and involvement (see Junker 1960: 36). But is participation necessarily such a dangerous, or at least diverting, activity in observation? Perhaps, as Jorgensen suggests, non-participation has an even greater capacity to miss the meaning of what we observe: 'the potential for misunderstanding and inaccurate observation increases when the researcher remains aloof and distanced physically and socially from the subject' (Jorgensen 1989: 56).

The fact is that most human observation of people (as distinct from trees or stars) necessarily involves some degree of participation and involvement. The researcher's question is not so much, 'should I become involved?' but rather 'what level and style of involvement and participation is appropriate, useful and acceptable in this particular situation?' As I have already indicated, the answer depends in part on what it is we wish to find out. But, because we are observing people not trees or stars, it also lies very much in the hands of our research subjects, who themselves become actively involved in shaping and guiding the style and focus of our observation. Certainly this has been my own experience.

Choosing participant observation

My New Guinea research project was an ethnographic description of beliefs and practices concerning health and illness in one village. In choosing this particular topic I thereby chose participant observation: living amongst the people, learning their language and the rhythms and patterns of their daily lives. In terms of Junker's model I intended to be an *observer as participant* in the hope of becoming a *participant as observer*. There was no alternative. But why, then, this topic? One reason was quite personal. Some years earlier, teaching in Nigeria, I had been made keenly aware of differences between Nigerian beliefs about illness and my own when roused from sleep by a noisy, lengthy tribal ritual which surrounded the house. Drumming and wailing sounds were at first to be heard some distance away and over a period of two or three hours gradually came to encircle the house and then finally dispersed. No one had given any warning that this might occur. Having read too many novels by Nicholas Monsarrat, we deduced from the fearsome noises that we were regarded as a source of danger, perhaps even seen as responsible for the cholera epidemic that was sweeping the area (the anti-cholera vaccine being stored in our fridge). The next day we learned from some villagers that we had, on the contrary, been treated to a powerful dose of preventative medicine.

The interest in these issues emerged at a more academic level a couple of years later when, now a postgraduate student in Sociology at Reading University, I was asked to discuss a paper by Robin Horton entitled 'African traditional thought and western science'. Part of its argument is that both systems of thought are primarily theoretical attempts to explain the world, thus casting doubt 'on most of the well-worn dichotomies used to conceptualise the differences: . . . intellectual versus emotional; rational versus mystical . . . empirical versus non-empirical; abstract versus concrete; analytical versus non-analytical' (Horton 1974: 152). I was attracted to Horton's perspective which asserted a basic intellectual equality underlying cultural difference and resisted the temptation of projecting on to the other (non-western belief systems) repressed, denied or forgotten dimensions of ourselves. The notion of equality has been important to me as long as I can remember; connected with being the youngest child perhaps, or coming from a working-class area and attending one of the first Comprehensive schools, though the idea was generally very much in the air in the 1950s and 1960s anyway.

To develop this interest in non-western belief systems and the way in which we understand other cultures, I moved over to Social Anthropology, which also involved moving over from red-brick Reading to the ivory towers of Oxford. Here I learnt the meaning of culture shock in a new way. I was different and at a disadvantage; I encountered privilege and patriarchy directly for the first time. How might a commuting, fairly hard-working, state-educated, mother of two small children fit in a system in which the real academic discussions took place over port or 'pot' in the evening. Moreover the theoretical underpinning of Reading style sociology and Oxford social anthropology in the 1970s themselves seemed to belong to two different belief systems; the former was based on Weber and Simmel, the latter on Evans-Pritchard and Levi-Strauss. The possibility of going into the field sounded infinitely preferable. I had my eye on a strongly egalitarian society at a considerable distance from Oxford elitism. Papua New Guinea beckoned.

Of course, none of this thinking featured in my research funding application, but I mention it now because it certainly shaped my decision-making. Over recent years there has emerged amongst anthropologists some awareness that the researcher's autobiography inevitably and rightly 'relates to the anthropological enterprise, which includes the choice and area of study, the experience of fieldwork, analysis and writing' (Okely 1992: 1).

At the time, the way in which I tended to explain my research focus emphasized my interest in the relationship between different belief systems and went something like this: Previous research in the Tolai area of New Guinea (e.g. Epstein 1969; Salisbury 1970) had revealed a remarkable ability to combine indigenous and western ways of life – whether economic, political, educational or religious – in a manner that allowed the persistence of a strong cultural identity and, to the outsider, raised questions about how people managed to live with such contradictory practices and world views. I wanted to work in such an area and, in particular, in a village that was economically traditional, yet had easy access to formal western health care. If villagers both retained their indigenous beliefs and also used formal health care to their advantage, research into how this worked would have important implications for professional understanding of health care. In short, perhaps it is possible to offer western health care without destroying cultural identity and to provide primary health care 'based on feasible modern scientific knowledge and health technologies as well as accepted and effective traditional healing practice' (WHO 1976: 44).

That I should have explained my research in an impersonal way is hardly surprising. By and large anthropologists have tended to split autobiography and anthropology, using diaries to off-load their isolation and frustration at the messy reality of fieldwork. (See for example the famous and fascinating Malinowski Diary (1967) that scandalized many of his followers.)

The notion that anthropologists should become objects for scrutiny 'in the same way that our research has rendered "objects" those other selves with whom we have interacted in the field' (Crick 1992: 175) was not in evidence amongst the anthropologists who taught me in Oxford in 1976. Neither was it present in the ethnographies I read at that time. Indeed the training was such that I encountered only polished and seemingly disembodied ethnography or very abstract theoretical works.

Within this milieu it is hardly surprising that the question of what sort of methods I should use in my research was something I hardly asked myself. There was no seminar on research methods and I assumed that as far as possible one just 'went native', learnt the language, watched, listened and wrote down everything that happened and was said. Perhaps this vagueness is to some extent part and parcel of anthropological fieldwork. A recent American textbook on research methods comments:

> Participant observation is the foundation of anthropological research, and yet it is the least well-defined methodological component of our discipline. It involves establishing rapport in a community, learning to act so that people go about their business as usual when you show up . . . to a certain extent participant observation must be learned in the field.
>
> (Russell Bernard 1988: 148)

Learning participant observation

From the start, things turned out to be more difficult than the elegant Oxford ethnographies had indicated. Visiting the university and research institute in the capital, Port Moresby, I discovered that anthropologists were not entirely welcome. Expressing the views of a group of indigenous social science students, one academic summed up their perceptions thus, 'More and more people are beginning to see through the anthropological mystique . . . the relationship [between anthropologist and the local population] is one of grossly unequal exchange, whether the relevant values be seen in material, moral or intellectual terms' (Gordon 1978: 7). Then I learnt my research permit couldn't be found; I was warned that to begin work without it could lead not only to my extradition, but also that of all other anthropologists in the area. Nine months later it still had not appeared so I ignored the warnings and, thankfully, no one was extradited. Keenly conscious of my guest status I proceeded with immense caution.

Local leaders suggested I should speak to a village meeting to gain the consent and understanding of that village. How was I to explain myself? I had found that people expected white women who went into villages to be nuns or teachers; they came to offer something – usually lessons in sewing or cake baking – not to learn. However, there had been one woman anthropologist in the area and she, they said, had been learning the language and writing a book. I tried to use their knowledge of her as my introduction and then added that I was especially interested to learn about health and illness. (For a fuller discussion of the difficulties encountered in explaining research, see Chapter 3 by Jan Walmsley). As I didn't yet know the Tolai language well, but spoke fluent Melanesian Pidgin, (a rough and ready Lingua-franca and product of the colonial encounter) I planned to speak to the meeting in Pidgin which would be translated into Tolai.[1] My attempt to speak through a woman from a neighbouring village proved an unwelcome introduction to rules about who may speak to whom and when. Faced with the mixed assembly the woman simply hung her head and refused to say a word. A young man came to my rescue interpreting each of my sentences freely and expansively including my request to move into the village. The outcome: I received agreement to *visit* the village once a fortnight. Feeling I hadn't been properly represented I decided to make the visits residential. Where to stay was the next question, but before I had a chance to utter it, the answer arrived in the form of Ia Pitini. I would be staying with her family she told me (she had eight children though only three remained at home) – and I would become her sister. (This kind of experience may be quite common. See, for example, Lederman 1986: 365 who was 'adopted' by a twelve-year-old boy.) I gratefully moved into her two-room bamboo-on-stilts home. One sleeping room was for males, one for females. For the next two years I spent about two-thirds of my time based at her home and one third with my own family in a very different kind of house some twenty miles down the road.

My chief informant had chosen me because, orphaned as a child, she had been for a while fed by Swiss nuns. She felt friendly towards my white skin and sensed I might be able to offer her something in return. The relationship was never formalized, and I'm not sure how equal the exchange seemed from her end, though my presence certainly meant she received better health care at the hospital and health centre. From my end she provided a home and the right to be in the village as well as great deal of friendship and wisdom.

My plan was to become directly involved in people's lives – listening to their conversations; accompanying them to the fields, the forest, and going with them to the market, the health centre, and to traditional specialists in herbal remedies and those with knowledge of sorcery. The women were impressively friendly and patient, the men more distant and preoccupied. It soon became clear that most of my time would be spent with the women.

At one level things seemed to be going well: I seemed to have been easily accepted. But after five or six months, I also began to panic. How was I to move from benevolent acceptance to inside understanding? There were two main difficulties. The first was my slowness in learning the language. After a year I could make myself understood but frequently failed to follow general conversation unless people spoke deliberately to me, which meant that I was conducting interviews rather than observing, or joining in, natural conversations. I couldn't both act as a fly on the wall and at the same time grasp the meanings. The possibility that this might be a common experience for anthropologists didn't occur to me at the time, though there are now indications that this may well be the case:

> Whereas at the moment it is conventional both to expect and claim that 'the anthropologist mastered the native language', it would be more balanced to say that both the expectation and the claim are unrealistic, and that the most accurate way of describing the ethnographic enterprise is to say that fieldworkers characteristically do *not* achieve much competence in the native language.
>
> (Campbell 1989: 19)

A second problem was a growing awareness that my acceptability to the women and their willingness to speak about things that were regarded as women's knowledge seemed to carry with it an expectation that I would not switch roles and talk with the men. 'If you really want to learn our way of life' they would say, 'you must behave the way we do'. I realized later that these women were, in effect, challenging a long-standing bias amongst anthropologists, aptly summarized in the assumption that women anthropologists tend to become 'honorary males'. Reiter describes how this assumption is perpetuated:

> we think that men control the significant information in other cultures . . . we search them out and tend to pay little attention to the women. Believing that men are easier to talk to, more involved in the crucial cultural spheres, we fulfil our own prophesies in finding them to be better informants
>
> (Reiter 1975: 14)

Edwin Ardener's analysis of male bias in fieldwork goes further. Also writing in 1975 he proposed a theory of 'muted groups', arguing that indigenous women's voices tend not to be heard and represented in anthropology because their model of reality, their view of the world, cannot be expressed using the terms of the male model dominant in their own culture and also dominant in the discipline of anthropology (Ardener 1975: 5).[2]

I was observing a great deal and, language permitting, participating extensively. The notebooks were piling up in the corner of the hut alongside the family's traditional wealth (a huge coil of shell money) and a picture of the Virgin Mary. There was, however, very little about health and illness between the covers of my notebooks. I could ridge up the sweet potatoes like an expert, bargain in the market place and even chew betel nut with ease, but I knew next to nothing about what makes people healthy or what were seen as the causes and cures of illness. Eventually I decided to ask the women I knew best what to do.

Why weren't they interested in the one subject that I'd travelled across the world to learn about? What happened to sick people? I rarely came across any (though I had been involved in the ceremonies surrounding death, so evidently people did become very ill). Laughingly they explained they weren't deliberately concealing things; all they knew was that sometimes illness was caused by sorcery, sometimes there was no cause. If they fell ill they would try both the health centre and a traditional specialist to cover themselves on both fronts, though their vulnerable state meant they didn't want people to hear of their illness. If I wanted to learn about the traditional treatments, I would have to go and talk to the men who had been inducted into specialist, ritual knowledge that enabled them to cure (and, I think, cause) illness. These men not only had knowledge of herbal remedies but also of the incantations that accompany the use of plant materials. One Tolai writer has described such ritual specialists as having been accepted into an understanding which is said to affect perceptions and memory as well as to establish a link between people and ancestral spirits (Enos 1977).

I felt reassured to have been given this directive; perhaps it meant I wouldn't forfeit the women's trust by talking to these men. So I decided to change my research methods. A diffuse, unstructured, participant observation was to be complemented by a more rigorous, focused mix of interviews and observation. Energized by this unexpected bout of hard-head realism I set off to visit each of the men on the list.

Yet again, I met a brick wall. Some I never managed to meet however many times I went to their homes. The rest proved either uninterested or evasive. The friendliest agreed to take me into the forest to show me the plants he used. Each appointment we made he broke. I finally grasped what was happening. Knowledge was power so why risk losing any by sharing it with an outsider? Perhaps it was rather like asking a Medical Consultant to risk halving his earnings, or allowing a woman into a priestly sanctuary, or both. (For a development of this analogy see Peberdy 1988.)

What next? Time was running out: I had been in the village for over a year and though I had observed a great deal, very little of it seemed relevant to my goal. Thankfully, the women continued to befriend me, though they seemed to smile in an odd sort of way. Eventually I realized I needed to change my research goal to something it was possible to observe and learn about from the women.

The realization happened this way. We were in church after the Sunday Mass and the priest began to publicly castigate a particular woman for 'killing babies'. I woke up. How had he discovered the practice of infanticide when it was quite unknown to me? In fact he was referring to the use of the contraceptive injection depo-provera, something I'd heard was recommended at the Health Centre and which was said to carry much higher risks than other forms of contraceptive. Here was a real problem to investigate, a research subject the women might get something out of in return for their patient friendliness and trust.

Observation took on a new meaning. I observed responses to the news that a woman was pregnant; I sat in on the contraceptive clinic at the Health Centre and listened to the questions and advice; in the fields or at meal times I guided the conversation towards the discussion of children and why they were valued. I was told stories I suspect a male anthropologist would never have been told. I asked about traditional forms of fertility control and received detailed answers. I consulted birth records and studied the records held at the family planning clinic. Through this combination of methods a definite picture was emerging.

The research even took on a comparative aspect when I combined efforts with an anthropologist who was working in a village with much less land, a lower birth rate and a higher level of formal education. Together we wrote policy-oriented reports, for the provincial government and family planning service and academic papers for ourselves, (Bradley and Peberdy 1988). So all was not lost. But why had things not worked out in the first place? And in the process, what had I learnt about participant observation?

Reflecting on participant observation

Interests

I have reflected on my choice and change of topic. Research is in many senses a co-operative venture; one of the reasons the original project did not come to fruition was clearly because it was chosen without reference to the people on whom I would be dependent for information. Projects that rely heavily on participant observation need to be in tune with the interests of the research population as well as those of the researcher. The practice of medicine and the relationship between western and indigenous medicine was not something that concerned the Tolai women, so it is hardly surprising that information was hard to come by. In a different sense, neither was the research topic in the interest of the Tolai men who owned the traditional knowledge. Their knowledge was a source of power that brought not only income and status, but also protected them and their kin from the ill-intentions of enemies.

In contrast, in a society which placed great value on children and in which women had always practised some form of fertility control, there was a wealth of experience and conversation that interested both the women and me. Though the men were rather less forthcoming than the women, they were not directly hostile and some of the younger married men quite informative.

I have so far spoken of the co-operative nature of research as though in an entirely pragmatic sense; 'if they aren't interested you won't learn much'. But perhaps the pragmatic points to a deeper ethical issue. The liberal values underlying my curiosity about other belief systems were clearly not universal and self-evident. I needed also to pay attention to the values and goals of the people who allowed me to be their guest so that my research programme might include activities that would be of interest and benefit to these people. This is, of course, what actually happened, when my original plan was thwarted. Only after a period of getting to know people, establishing trust and learning (something) of the language is one in a position to identify what is or is not in other people's interests. What a research population is going to get out of my research activities is a question I would hope to have in the forefront of my mind, from start to finish, if I were to attempt this kind of research again. More widely, I suspect it is a question that ought to be asked in many other kinds of research too, though it certainly is of central importance for those of us who attempt participant observation in a society that has long experience of unequal exchange between black and white.

Detachment

It has often been suggested that the participant observer is attempting to combine both involvement and detachment. Writing in 1970, Louise and George Spindler describe the tension thus:

> The participant observer must be involved and detached at the same time – sympathetic and empathetic and objective . . . It is the participant observer role that eventually creates personal problems for the anthropologist as well as giving him(sic) the most important data he usually collects. The people become friends, and he frequently becomes virtually a member of the family, so to speak. It is not always easy to write about one's friends – The antidote is [a] special kind of objectivity.
> (Spindler and Spindler 1970: 288–9)

Was my earlier work lacking in such objectivity? I began as a member of a family, gradually acquired a network of friends and only towards the end began to act more like a data collector, conducting interviews and compiling statistics. But perhaps that family involvement and time spent in the fields, at the market, or sharing in the family cooking was as important as note-taking because fieldwork is a 'total experience, demanding all the anthropologists resources; intellectual, physical, emotional, political and intuitive. The experience involves so much of the self that it is impossible to reflect upon it fully by extracting that self' (Okely 1992: 8). In this view objectivity in the sense of detachment isn't possible; participant observation means learning through all the senses. 'We use this total knowledge to make sense literally of the recorded material . . . Fieldnotes may be no more than a trigger for bodily and hitherto subconscious memories' (1992: 16). Looking back I think this view is right, though at the time only part of me felt this might be so.

The methodological problem I encountered was not so much over-identification and lack of objectivity as a failure to structure the social contacts I developed by selecting a sample of families whom I would visit on a very regular (daily or weekly) basis. Relying on word-of-mouth or chance meetings in order to discover who was ill and what kinds of treatment they were seeking was an inappropriate way of keeping in touch with people who are ill, when illness tends to be dealt with by social withdrawal and silence. Reflecting on my experience of participant observation has highlighted the need to be focused and pro-active as well as participative and immersed in the general rhythms of daily life.

Being yourself

For quite a large part of my time, whilst waiting for permission to start field-work and even more so after I started, I tended to think how much easier it would all be if I were black and male. I was especially conscious of this when I pressed one of the Tolai men about his reluctance to discuss the question I was asking about indigenous medical beliefs. He said that he could begin to do so with my husband (who spoke no Tolai, had no training in anthropology and lived in comparative luxury some distance away) but not with me. Now this might have been an avoidance technique, I don't know. At the time it made me angry. It was part of the brick wall that forced me to retrace my steps and consider the kinds of knowledge to which I did have access.

Looking back, I think my expectations were to some extent overly influenced by the image of anthropologist as transcendent male, straining towards objectivity, when in fact participant observation is necessarily a fragile, inter-subjective enterprise in which our particular characteristics (in my case being female, white, part of the post-war baby-boom, a mother, rather slow at language learning, etc.) are 'simultaneously enabling and disabling' (Peshkin 1985: 278). These are essential parts of the picture, not secondary features, that have a tendency to get in the way.

What did the women observe of me? In one sense a great deal, for I was rarely allowed to be alone even when writing, reading or taking a wash (as much an expression of care-taking as of curiosity, I think). What they noticed and found curious, amusing, pleasing or distasteful I can only piece together from their laughter, questions and the way my presence was explained to strangers.

Trying to teach me to speak and act like a Tolai and then laughing at the mistakes was a game most of the women and some of the men clearly enjoyed and with a sense of pride at the occasional success. They correctly observed my desire to learn. It was unexpected questions that pointed to the gaps of which I had been unaware. Like the time Ia Pitini asked, 'Don't white women know how to cry?' I was thrown, until eventually I realized she didn't mean, 'Don't you have emotions?' but 'Why don't you women go in for public weeping as we do after a death?' In the end, what I *think* the women observed was some-one fairly like them, but less competent in many ways.

One final thought. Being observed can certainly feel threatening and intru-sive. Sometimes Ia Pitini decided to turn the tables by accompanying me to my own home and then just silently sitting, like a disapproving ghost, whilst we tried to get on with life as best we could. What she observed then I'd prefer not to know.

Notes

1. Pidgin was not an appropriate language in which to communicate with Tolai villagers. Not everyone spoke it, and it was looked down upon: 'for a Tolai to speak Pidgin is very comparable with an English speaker speaking Pidgin; they regard it as a substandard or 'bad' version of the 'real language' (Salisbury 1967: 46).
2. It is important to note that this awareness of the exclusion of women from public discourse was, in anthropology, a first step towards the development of more sophisticated approaches towards the study of gender (see Moore 1988).

5

Relating

Dorothy Atkinson

There are many more stories to be told and voices yet to be heard.

This quotation is the very last sentence of *Know Me As I Am*, an anthology of prose, poetry and art by people with learning difficulties (Atkinson and Williams 1990: 244). As co-editor of the anthology (with Fiona Williams), I wanted to take its ideas and some of its approaches further in some research of my own. We had suggested, in the anthology's conclusion, that the book might form the starting point of other people's research; so why not mine? The anthology was thus part of the inspiration, and the motivation, for the project I describe and explore below.

The anthology forms the starting point of this chapter on 'Relating', because I duly set out to compile more stories through listening to some of those voices. There is, however, more to telling – and hearing – people's accounts of their lives and experiences than simply providing a forum. The role of the researcher, or listener, has a bearing on how stories unfold and what they are about. The research interview is a social situation, and is influenced by the perceptions of its participants. This chapter takes as its theme the interpersonal dynamics of the research setting – in this case a group setting – and looks at how the key actors related to one another.

The project (which I use below as a case study) focused on the experiences of a group of older people with learning difficulties. Together they, and I, compiled an oral historical account of their lives, from childhood to adulthood. In doing so, at least within the group, their voices were heard and their experiences acknowledged. This places the project within the framework of qualitative research, where people's subjective experience of their social worlds is sought and recorded. In involving people with learning difficulties, the project makes a contribution to the growing self-advocacy movement, which also seeks to give people a voice. The focus on the past, and the group format, identifies this research more specifically as oral history. The three distinctive features of this research were that it concerned people with learning difficulties; it involved them both as individuals and as a group in developing an historical account of their lives; and it provided an opportunity for people to make sense of their experiences.

There is a growing interest in, and literature about, qualitative research in relation to people with learning difficulties. Increasingly, researchers are using interviews and other methods to find out and explore the viewpoints and experiences of people with learning difficulties. Other methods are being sought because even the specially adapted, informal and largely conversational research interview (Flynn 1986; Atkinson 1988) is not universally successful in enabling people to talk freely and openly about themselves. Thus the emphasis, in some quarters, has been on enhancing the informality of the contact, for example through getting to know people outside the research project (Jahoda et al. 1988) or adopting a naturalistic approach and spending time relaxing with respondents on social visits and outings (Edgerton 1984). Getting to know people by 'being there', alongside them, during ordinary and often boring days, has also been used as a means of capturing experiences at first hand (Wilkinson 1990).

Oral history involves people remembering, and recalling, past personal and social events and often includes people who have been neglected in traditional history books, such as working-class people, women and mental health survivors. (This point is developed more fully by Joanna Bornat in her chapter on 'Presenting'.) My own project aimed to involve a group of people with learning difficulties in the process of compiling an oral history of their lives. In doing so, it built on two other ventures in this area: the oral historical accounts featured in the anthology, *Know Me As I Am*, and the oral history of a long-stay hospital as witnessed and recalled by some of its older residents (Potts and Fido 1991).

This oral history project provided a place where people's stories – their own accounts of their lives – could be told and heard. This chapter looks at the process of that story-telling, and how the oral historians came to give their accounts. I also tell my story, my account of my own involvement in this process and how – often unwittingly – I helped influence its direction. How I presented myself, and how people saw me, were important factors in determining how we related to one another. These factors were often not obvious at the time. Indeed, it is only now, through a similar process of recall and reflection, that I can begin to make sense of my own experiences.

Relating to a wider context

In focusing on relating, this chapter is part of a recent but growing interest in the interpersonal dynamics of face-to-face research interviews. People who are involved in participative and feminist research, in particular, have begun to explore these encounters in terms of their capacity for avoiding, or reinforcing, the exploitation of potentially vulnerable people. The conscious move away from hierarchical research relationships (Oakley 1981), and the involvement of research participants in studies of their lives (Holman 1987; Graham 1984), have opened up opportunities for people to talk about themselves in an atmosphere which is both constructive and enabling. Most people welcome the opportunity to talk to an attentive and interested listener about their lives and personal experiences. Sometimes this can be an uplifting experience which gives people a sense of self-worth (Coleman 1986).

There are, however, possible pitfalls in this development. Even a consciously non-exploitative approach, which builds on trust between the researcher and the participants, can itself become the source of further exploitation. The research potential of a friendly and informal approach is considerable. People can, and do, confide their views, their concerns and experiences willingly to someone prepared to listen. But an atmosphere of trust, a relationship between 'equals' and the blurring of distinctions between the key actors can in themselves lead to expectations of a continuing friendship and a continuing involvement in the development of the research. There may be, at the end, a sense of loss or betrayal when the research relationship is terminated, and the researcher moves on (Finch 1984; Patai 1991), usually with the research (Stacey 1991). The research experience can be, and often is, a positive experience for its participants. The researcher needs to bear the pitfalls in mind, however, and build in safeguards against them. It is also important to take steps to ensure that the research experience carries with it a sense of achievement rather than loss. An awareness of the interpersonal dynamics of the interview situation is a first step, including the recognition that this is an 'emotionally charged' situation for a respondent receiving undivided attention (Patai 1991).

There is more than an echo here of the psychoanalytic or psychotherapeutic process, in that strong feelings may be unleashed which need careful and sensitive handling to ensure a positive outcome. Life history and oral history work, in particular, can incorporate the therapeutic effects of remembering, and opportunities to reflect on a personal past can lead to a stronger sense of self in the present (Thompson 1988). The feeling of being affirmed and validated in the research process can be further developed through the product of the research, especially if the product is a publication which 'gives a voice' to people otherwise unheard.

The project

Aims

When I started this project my primary aim was to *explore a method* (use of oral history techniques), in relation to a particular client group, (people with learning difficulties). My interest in this approach, and this group, has its origins in two earlier projects. Some years ago I completed a follow-up study of people who had left long-stay mental handicap hospitals in Somerset to live in the community. This project had involved one-off interviews with 50 respondents (Atkinson 1988) and had convinced me that people with learning difficulties do have stories to tell. This knowledge was further reinforced by the work involved in co-editing the anthology, *Know Me As I Am*. The anthology began to show the exciting possibilities of life story and oral history, work with people with learning difficulties, and to demonstrate that in-depth interviewing with a few people could have as much (if not more) impact as single interviews with larger numbers of respondents. I was hooked. I wanted to explore for myself the oral history approach.

As part of my Somerset research, I had produced an illustrated booklet of research findings for respondents so that everyone had a personal record of the research to refer to afterwards. Similarly, the anthology contributors each received personal copies of the book in recognition of their work, as a keepsake of the project. I planned from the outset, therefore, that the oral historians involved in this project would likewise receive a written product at the end – a compilation of their stories. This was not an aim of the project itself – as I saw it – but more a by-product of our joint labours. This is not how it turned out in practice, as I explain below, as the group developed its own aims which included developing 'Our Book'.

The group

The group consisted of nine people; seven men and two women. The age range was 57 to 77, with most people in their late sixties or early seventies. I approached potential members via special services, so that the actual oral historians were all drawn from residential and day settings. The project, initially seen (by me) as lasting a few weeks, in fact lasted for almost two years. The acute worry I confided in my diary at the outset ('How can I retain their interest?') soon became, and remained, a more chronic anxiety ('How will it ever end?'). The group, it seemed, had a life and momentum of its own, in spite of my efforts to impose boundaries on its work and limit its lifespan.

My agenda

I was interested in finding ways and means of enabling people with learning difficulties to talk freely, and openly, about their experiences. In particular, I was interested in their narrative accounts of their lives during some of the major legislative and policy changes of this century. This included the effects of the eugenics movement, and the incarceration of people in institutions. I was also interested in more recent moves to community care, and what sort of impact this might have had on their lives.

I wanted to explore this history 'from below'. There was a very real dilemma, however, about how to work with people in the group to achieve this aim. An immediate and direct approach might jeopardize the whole project. Indeed, I had been advised by staff who knew individual members well to proceed with caution in revealing potentially painful layers of hospital memories. It seemed to me, at that time, that the direct approach could lead in either of two equally problematic directions. On the one hand it could lead us all into a cul-de-sac if, when people discovered that they were expected to reveal painful memories to a stranger, and in a group setting, they then refused to do so. On the other hand, there was the possibility that people would all too readily engage in this process and, in the course of it, *would* get in touch with past memories and thereby release long-hidden feelings of frustration and anger. And then what?

All in all, directness seemed too great a risk. I chose what seemed at the time the safest course of action. I would avoid early and direct questioning about group members' specific experiences as people labelled, treated and segregated in special settings for people with learning difficulties. For almost everyone, this had included often quite extended periods of incarceration in long-stay hospitals. Instead of focusing on the experiences which they shared and which were quite different from my own, I decided – for pragmatic reasons – to focus on ordinary memories, such as family memories and accounts of childhood, schooldays and everyday village or town life.

The approach I had chosen reflected my interest in, and commitment to, the whole person. I was pleased with it. It would enable people to relate to, and engage in, memories of a universal kind and, no doubt, a richer and more rounded history would emerge as a result. At the same time I was being protective of everyone, including myself; sparing us from depressing accounts of life in long-stay hospitals, at least in our early days. They would emerge, I hoped, in the fullness of time.

This was my agenda. In the end it worked, but not in the way I had envisaged. Whilst Barry (no real names are used in this account) was happy to describe his back-to-back house in Yorkshire and the cobbled streets of his home-town, other people's memories of their own childhood homes were inextricably linked with memories of earlier loss, separation and rejection. Inevitably, the focus on childhood led to the disclosure of personal suffering. In contrast, later memories of adult life in an institution, because shared, were often told with humour and in a spirit of defiance. Somehow I had lost sight of a simple fact; memories of an unhappy childhood can be more painful than accounts of adult life in a long-stay hospital. In reality I could not protect people from their pasts, nor should I have tried.

The researcher's role

How I introduced myself

This was a 'history' group. That was how I described it in informal meetings with potential participants beforehand; and how I explained it to staff. It became known as the history group in the residential home where we held our meetings.

I introduced myself to the group as someone from the Open University, who was interested in history and who was thinking of writing a book on historical events. Their memories of times gone by would be an important source of information for this book. This explanation given and reiterated in the early meetings was accepted and understood. I also introduced my tape recorder at the first meeting. It was regarded with some interest initially, and group members listened to re-played snatches of conversation in that first meeting. It was never mentioned again, so it seemed as if people accepted its presence thereafter.

The history group initially met weekly, and quickly became a familiar and predictable event in people's lives. It also became seen as a place to have fun – where repartee, wit and humour could be engaged to defuse painful memories. It became something to look forward to. It was an unpopular decision, two years later, when I drew it to a close.

What I had in mind

Prior to our first meeting, and with the help of two colleagues, I drew up a list of themes to explore within the group. These included the sort of houses people lived in and where they were situated; what their neighbours and their neighbourhoods were like; and how they cooked, washed and kept warm. I included discussions about families – family size and composition, and family relationships. I hoped to uncover personal memories but also period details of the time; descriptions of the clothes people wore, for example, and what happened on wash-days. At each group meeting I was accompanied by one or two staff members from the residential or day settings who knew at least some of the participants well. They pursued and reinforced the chosen topics; joining in with personal reminiscences, where appropriate, but also drawing people out and helping to translate and interpret their responses. In a sense, staff acted as role models. Their willingness to join in, and review their own lives, probably encouraged other people to do likewise.

My own task, as I saw it, was to provide a safe and friendly environment in which people would feel free to talk about their earlier life experiences. I took on the role of a friendly, but distant, group facilitator. I asked questions, and reflected on what was said, but I did not, on the whole, join in the reminiscences. The idea was to spend time in the early days on safe topics, so that people not only gained confidence in themselves, but they would also begin to trust me and each other sufficiently to confide more personal memories later.

I saw myself as responsible for this group, because it had been established at my instigation and reflected my aims, agenda and assumptions. This responsibility was expressed through control. I controlled the group's agenda, and chose the topics to explore – or I attempted to.

What everyone else had in mind

My control was always tenuous. I might bring up topics and persist with them, and sometimes they would strike an answering chord. But often they did not. Group sessions often left me feeling out of control and powerless, as topics were sabotaged through side conversations, stage whispers, loud yawns, interruptions and the accomplished telling of extended anecdotes (on rival themes).

Yet I continued to see myself as potentially powerful in that setting. I knew that the participants had encountered powerful women in their lives before, and I assumed, therefore, that I would be seen as one in a long line of potential or actual oppressors. My safe environment/safe topics policy and my friendly demeanour were meant to counteract that image. Looking back now, I think the tactics worked – at least for everyone else. My powerful-person image, however, stayed in my own mind. Thus it was, I think, that the group and I proceeded along different, though linked, paths. They perceived me as I appeared, as a friendly and interested person – not as I feared (through a process of transference) as a powerful person. They actually believed what they saw, and treated me – at times – as their confidante, a kind of 'benefactor' in Edgerton's terms (Edgerton 1967).

It is obvious now, with the benefit of hindsight, that group members had role models other than the powerful-woman image. People varied as to what sort of benefactor they took me to be, and I was variously related to as a friend, a co-conspirator or, simply, as an interested 'young' woman. Thus I was teased rather than deferred to, and flirted with rather than feared. Nods, winks and smiles were more likely than an anxious frown.

Group members' individual perceptions of me as a basically friendly person led inevitably to early, even cheerful, disclosures. In the first three sessions, for example, amidst and around my 'safe' topics, group members themselves tried to introduce a range of unsafe areas. These included being put away as children; abuse; separation and loss; deaths; and admission to hostels and hospitals. Group members were actually more interested in revealing their personal pasts, than in building a joint history of earlier times. They were, from the outset, open about themselves and willing to share painful memories. Their agenda, it seemed, was to talk about, and make sense of, their personal pasts and histories. My agenda was to stop them – and, in so doing, to try and protect them from their pasts.

The research process

What I did in the group

My sense of responsibility for this group, and its members, prompted many of my actions and reactions during the early months of the project. I felt responsible, as I said earlier, for protecting people from their own pasts and their personal feelings. But it did not end there. I also felt responsible for the atmosphere in group meetings so that people would feel comfortable, relaxed and valued. I felt responsible for the content of our discussions, and saw it as my task to think of themes or, as this got more difficult, to acquire reminiscence aids such as tapes, slides and photographs, to act as memory triggers. I felt responsible for keeping the group going, and maintaining people's interest. Later on, it became apparent, I duly became responsible for the group's therapeutic function and tried to ensure that people were not overwhelmed by sadness and regret.

This is a lot of responsibility, and it weighed heavily. It meant I was not always open to what was actually happening, and often I would misunderstand, miss cues or misinterpret what (I thought) I heard. I pursued my agenda, when other people had their own. My perception of my role and my tasks often conflicted with what other people perceived. These perceptions helped determine how we related to one another.

As the group's facilitator *and* its protector, my role varied between opening up and exploring some topics whilst ignoring and closing down others. I illustrate this below, with an extract taken from the tape transcript of our second meeting. It entails an exchange between myself (D) and Enid:

D: Right, so if you can all think back to when you were children; can you remember what sort of house you used to live in?

E: I used to live up Farley Hill with my mum before she died

D: And what sort of house was that?

E: Well, a big one.

D: A big one?

E: Yes. A big one, up Farley Hill, yes.

D: Up Farley Hill.

E: Yes.

D: Was that in . . . ?

E: In Luton, yes. Then I had to come to the hostel.

D: Right. And can you tell me about the house? What was it like?

My theme was 'type of house', and I pursued it regardless of Enid's mention, first, of her mother's death and, second, of going to live in a hostel. She may have been ready to talk, but I was far from ready to listen. Two other ways of 'relating' are illustrated in this extract. I frequently asked questions, aiming to show interest and draw people out; and I reflected back their comments, as a means of checking my understanding of what was said.

I became very aware of asking questions and often felt like an interrogator. Whilst sometimes I wished it could be more of a conversation, my sense of responsibility for content and direction spurred me on. Yet, on those few occasions when I said something simple and personal ('I was never very good at skipping') it became more like a conversation ('Poor Dorothy!' 'Oh, what a shame') and moved the group on.

Counsellors and therapists consciously use reflective techniques to enable clients to gain awareness and insight into their own behaviour and actions. I used reflective techniques too, and they almost certainly helped the group meetings become therapeutic. However, I used reflection for very practical reasons. The speech of most participants was unclear; that fact combined with mildly anarchic group behaviour (where two or three people spoke at once or, worse, everyone spoke together) meant I had difficulty understanding what was said. I began to reflect back in the hope of clarifying meanings there and then but, failing that, I would have a second chance later when I transcribed the tape. In one sense my echoing comments were a means of relating to the speaker at the time, but in another sense they were a means of speaking to myself on tape. They sometimes led nowhere, however, as the following extract illustrates:

D: What sort of gardening did you do, Jim?
J: I used to work on the proper garden.
D: The proper garden?
J: In the greenhouse and that.
D: So you worked in the greenhouse . . .
J: I did a lot more than that.
D: More than that?
J: Yes.

What everyone else did in the group

I had my agenda (usually reinforced by staff), but group members had their own. Three such individual agendas recurred throughout the meetings. First, there were topics which individuals wanted to pursue, and which they persisted with, often against the odds. These were people's *personal agendas* and were obviously very important. Unfortunately I did not always hear what individual members were trying to say (see the extract below). Second, people had personal secrets, areas of their lives which they did not want to disclose. These *areas of privacy* were kept under wraps even when individuals were pursued and closely questioned (see examples 1, 2, and 3 in the first extract on p. 67). And, third, a fine narrative tradition began to emerge – for whoever regaled the group with *an extended personal anecdote* was able to hold the floor and determine the content and direction of the overall discussion. These anecdotes, as I mentioned in passing earlier, were often on rival themes. In a sense, they were an expression of personal rivalry; a bid for at least temporary leadership of the group (see the second extract on p. 67).

Setting a personal agenda

This extract is taken from the third meeting. Enid has already attempted to talk about her mother's death and about her experience of being 'put away' as a child. Here she tries again:

E: I used to live with my mum and then she went out one night, and she got knocked down by a car, so she had to go to hospital to have cataracts on her eyes and then she died.
D: Oh dear.
E: But I used to do all the housework and everything, do her shopping for her, go out with her every Saturday night.
D: What sort of age were you then?
E: I was only younger.
D: You were younger than you are now?
E: Yes.
D: Were you a very young child? At that stage. Or was that later?
E: No, that was when I was fourteen.
D: Right. So when you were very young, did you have your own room? Because you were a very large family, from what you were saying last week . . .
E: Yeah, I can't remember, 'cos I was put away, see.

D: Yes, I remember that . . . Can anyone else remember? Did you have your own room?

Maintaining areas of privacy

In later group meetings, Bob revealed a lot about his home and family. In the early days, however, he was reluctant to talk about his childhood and effectively blocked well-meaning efforts to draw him out. The following examples are taken from our third meeting.

Example 1
J: (staff) Did you have any brothers and sisters Bob?
B: I don't worry about them.
J: Did you have any though?

Example 2
D: Can you remember your neighbours Bob?
B: What?
D: Who used to live next door?
B: No, no.

Example 3
M: (staff) You were telling me this morning how old your mother was when she died . . .
D: How old was she?
B: I can't tell you.

Narrating personal anecdotes

The knack of holding the floor with a well-chosen personal anecdote emerged early on in the group's life, and quite quickly became an established feature. Over time, the narrative structure became quite complex, but in the early days, in the first three or four meetings, these accounts were relatively short and straightforward. The well-told anecdote became a tradition in the group; the following tale, by Godfrey, is an early example.

> He [a teacher] comes round to me and clips me round the earhole. I says: 'Enough of that mister!' He says: 'What are you going to do about it?' I said: 'If you keep hitting me, you'll see.' He didn't live far from where I used to live so I told me dad, and me dad went to see him after. He said: 'That's enough of clipping my lad's earhole. If anybody can do that, I can, not you. You leave his ear alone!'

Outcomes

At a point in the group's own history, (it turned out to be the mid-point), there was a change of ownership. My agenda was replaced by theirs. This came as a great relief to me as it lessened, perhaps even removed, my sense of responsibility. The change occurred because as meeting followed meeting, and transcript followed transcript, I became increasingly aware that – in spite of everything – there was a product in the making. During the summer of our first year, we took a break from meetings to allow me time to compile the fragments, vignettes and anecdotes into a coherent whole.

Thus it was that, when we met again, I was able to hand everyone a personal copy of a large-print reprographed booklet with a coloured cover. This was entitled *Past Times*, but that was my title (Atkinson 1991). To everyone else it became known as Our Book. This one act of reciprocity on my part transformed how we related within the group. The delight in the book as it was, and the desire to make it bigger and better, proved potent forces. The book became a trigger to its own contributors, as I spent most of my time from now on giving readings from Our Book. The readings evoked a response in everyone, leading people to reveal more and more layers of memories, including painful ones.

It was evident, even then, that a change had occurred in the group dynamics. The catalyst for this was the book, and it led to important changes of perception all round. Members of the group increasingly saw me as a useful person as well as a nice one. I, in turn, came to see them as custodians of valuable individual and social histories, but generous custodians who were willing to share their knowledge. In retrospect, the work we did together subsequently on Our Book represented the coming-together of the two agendas: my agenda, to build a collective account – and theirs, to tell personal stories and reveal individual histories.

Our Book could do both. Put together, their individual accounts carry a stronger message. They highlight and reinforce important period details and point up universal themes. But this historical account is told through the individual voices of the group members. Every thought, idea and observation in Our Book is attributed to a person. The pride people felt in the product of our work was two-fold; they were proud of their *personal* contribution, however modest, but they were also exceedingly proud of the document as a whole, both in terms of its overall size and the richness of its content. Thus, in time, their *collective* effort came to be valued too. (In a sense, the putting together of the book represents the usual research process of aggregating data. The whole then says something different from the individual parts, a phenomenon which Moyra Sidell grapples with in her chapter on 'Interpreting'.)

The readings continued over the months that followed, and the layers of memories steadily peeled away. Inevitably Our Book became Our Second Book and finally Our Third Book. In a sense, the outcome of this project was good; people have a product to be proud of. More stories *were* told and voices *were* heard. But people had to *struggle* to tell their stories and have them heard. My well-meaning attempts to protect people from their own pasts, and from themselves, were unwarranted. They did not need protecting from me either. I was certainly controlling, but never powerful. Group members persisted in seeing me – in spite of my efforts – as essentially benign and harmless. They related to me as a personal confidante, not as a latter-day ward sister, and rightly refused to be tyrannized.

Postscript

Does the successful development of an unpublished booklet (*Past Times*) represent a universally good outcome for this project? At the time I really thought so. Indeed, even previous drafts of this chapter have ended with the paragraph above and the assumed good outcome or – as colleagues saw it – the classically happy ending to my story of the research. Was there a good outcome? And was it really a happy ending?

It was a good outcome in that *Past Times* (or Our Book) was produced, and duly celebrated. But it remains unpublished. It may be a rich account of people's individual and shared experiences, but it has yet to find a wider audience through a mainstream publisher. This is a disappointment. Group members were spurred on in our later meetings by the thought of communicating with people beyond their immediate circles, but this has not happened. (In her chapter 'Telling', Sally French explores the many difficulties of finding a publisher.)

I brought the group to an end. It was a 'happy ending' for me (and probably for staff members who were involved in organizing transport) but not necessarily for anyone else. Group meetings had, for almost two years, provided a forum in which people could recall and relate events and experiences from their past lives. The group was valued and the shared (and articulated) wish was for it to continue – indefinitely. I drew it to an end in spite of protests and pleas. In a very real sense, then, this could be seen as an *unhappy* ending, with the termination of the group's life and the subsequent loss of friendships.

Finding better ways of relating to one another in a research project is all well and good. It is a strategy which encourages relationships to build and trust to develop between the people involved. In this case, it also meant that group members came to enjoy the process itself, and got a lot out of relating to one another and relating their own accounts of past events and experiences. Perhaps, therefore, the ending of the group's life, when it came, was actually quite painful.

This postscript forms a new and less-than-happy ending to my own story. It is based on a more self-critical and reflective analysis of events and my part in them. The entirely positive glow has gone. What I saw *then* is tempered now by what I, and others, have seen since. Responsibility for research continues up to and including its ending. This is a salutary conclusion to reach. And a painful one to reflect on.

Acknowledgements

I wish to thank all the people who took part in this project. This includes both the oral historians themselves and the staff who worked alongside them. My thanks are to everyone for their generous investment of time, energy and enthusiasm to this project.

6

Sharing

Ann Brechin

Every approach needs to presume upon its reception. And so, in beginning we never fear that we shall be wholly misunderstood: we trust that our hesitancy, our stumbling talk, and our choice of words are not a search in the dark. To begin is confidently part of the work of building and sharing an understanding.

(O'Neill 1975: 1)

This chapter is about embarking on collaborative research. It is about working together with people who would conventionally be seen as the passive subjects of the research. It is about attempting to develop research questions together, exploring agendas and issues, and clarifying meanings. It is perhaps most like working with an advisory group at the stage where the research questions are still being negotiated, only in this case the advisory group members are people with learning disabilities.

With the help of a social worker acting as intermediary, seven individuals with learning disabilities were invited to take part in discussions about Shared Action Planning.[1] I explained to them that I wanted to do some research to find out how Shared Action Planning worked in practice and that these discussions would help me *plan* the research. Even I, who had set the project up, found this a difficult two-tier purpose to grasp. Jan Walmsley's chapter 'Explaining' explores well the complexity of such problems. Nonetheless, six meetings took place in 1990.

Creating a context in which relatively abstract issues could be meaningfully discussed presented particular challenges and dilemmas and, in practical terms, took a considerable amount of time. And this was only to get to first base – to arrive at an agreed framework of research questions around which a research project might subsequently be developed. As the meetings progressed, however, it began to feel as if the process took over from the purpose. Setting up the group, creating a friendly relaxed environment in which ideas could be shared had been seen as the process required in order to arrive at an agreed research agenda. The reality proved more complex. The sharing process took over and developed its own impetus, becoming, in effect, an end in itself.

What did this mean for my role as researcher? If I was really committed to sharing should I have been prepared to simply let things unfold? Or should I remain partly outside, watchful and responsive, involved, but remembering my purpose? My purpose, then, appeared to be to set limits on the sharing, to define the boundaries. Dorothy Atkinson in her chapter on 'Relating', describes similar uncertainties. Whether this was good or bad is still unclear to me. The relationships remained unequal, as in most research, and the sharing was largely on my terms. And yet it seemed an essential and valuable starting point.

Why sharing?

'Why sharing as a theme?' probed a colleague after reading a first draft of this chapter. 'I'd like an explanation of how you developed an interest in this approach.' As Fiona Williams suggests in her chapter 'Thinking', such questions seem necessary to give permission to explore self-motivation more deeply. What was it that made me do it? What kinds of academic arguments or research traditions convinced me to take on such a venture? Were there other factors too, stemming from my personal belief system or my style of operating as an individual?

Such questions are not easy to answer. This is partly because, even here in a book setting out to reveal in some sense the truth behind formal research accounts, we can still be selective in what we choose to reveal and how we tell our stories. Indeed we may well not fully understand them ourselves. The following explanation is my retrospective attempt to make sense of how I came to be involved in Sharing.

Scientific method

As a psychology student, 25 years ago, I had no particular difficulty with grasping the established scientific method. The tightness of its formulations, the logical discipline involved, the statistics, etc. did not alienate me. In fact it rather appealed to me. I believed, and still believe, in a necessary scepticism and a readiness to suspect the validity or reliability of research findings.

I have embraced only gradually the challenges to the positivist scientific method, contained in books such as this (and outlined in more detail in the Introduction) and the alternative methodologies in the social sciences. Qualitative research, symbolic interactionism and postmodernism seem fundamental to me now and will not go away. Yet I still believe that to ask, 'What is the likelihood that this outcome has any significance, either statistically or in terms of its meaningfulness or importance?' is to raise doubts about a great deal of apparently respectable research, whether qualitative or quantitative.

Hammersley (1989) presents a critical analysis of the qualitative method, suggesting that despite the compelling advantages, it still fails to demonstrate that it can qualify for the status of a scientific research methodology. It fails, he suggests, to produce replicable evidence in support of claims – a fundamental requirement of any measure of demonstrable and generalizable truth.

My early difficulties with the scientific method were not therefore that I had the foresight to reject it in favour of alternatives. The trouble was – well, there were several sources of trouble.

Reservations and grand concerns

I always felt uncomfortable asking people to do me the favour of acting as research subjects. I felt doubtful about the validity or morality of my claim on their time. Could I really justify it? It was true that they didn't mind, and they could refuse. I think they also quite enjoyed it, on the whole. But they assumed it must be important and worthwhile and accorded me the status I took upon myself (or was supposed to take on myself) of someone who could request their co-operation for my own ends (or the pursuit of knowledge, maybe). Looking back I think I carried and still carry today two sets of rather grand concerns, which fit very comfortably within current research paradigms, but which are somewhat in conflict with the scientific method and have been strangely paralysing.

The first concern was that there can be no certainties. Recognizing that other's viewpoints will differ and yet have their own validity, and that all attempts to impose meaning are open to challenge and alternative explanations was something I grasped early. Simplistic accounts did not exist in the socially aware, professional family into which I was born. What derived from this was not so much a useful methodological framework as a habitual sense of doubt. It amounted to more than a healthy scepticism and seemed more like a lack of solid ground from which to start.

Such ideas are, of course, now well-embedded in a number of evolving research methodologies and academic debates. The introduction to this book acknowledges, for example, the significant contribution of feminist research to the process of identifying new agendas and methodologies which start from the perspective of women themselves. A significant emphasis on qualitative as opposed to quantitative research has underpinned such developments. This brings with it a central recognition of the extent to which realities are created through negotiated meanings rather than through objective measurement. It also makes explicit the sense in which such processes are political; those who hold the power can control the definitions of truth.

Discussing research into violence against women, for example, Hanmer and Leonard state:

> What now appears as a new theory of knowledge – viz: that to understand
> the phenomena you must start with the perspective of those who are

subordinated – came from consciousness raising in the Women's Liberation Movement and gained much from other social welfare movements.

(Hanmer and Leonard 1984: 50)

The second of my grand concerns has, I think, been a determination to
strive for social justice and equality on behalf of oppressed or vulnerable
groups. Again, this must stem in part from my family of birth, with a
generations-old history of standing up for people's rights, and an espousal of
socialism at a time when it was distinctly unfashionable. This sense of social
responsibility was further compounded by an awareness of personal privilege
and resultant guilt. The unspoken rule I think I derived from this conviction,
was that only actions which contributed in some way to the welfare of others
(particularly oppressed others) were legitimate. This eliminated a lot of
possibilities.

Approaches which do offer a way of acknowledging such concerns now have
a high profile, reflected, for example, in the contents of this book. The chapters
by Dorothy Atkinson and Joanna Bornat both describe research which gives a
voice through the development of biographical accounts of people's lives.
Such approaches (for example, Bogdan and Taylor 1982; Holman 1987; Atkinson and Williams 1990) along with the growing work on supporting self-
advocacy with vulnerable or oppressed people (for example, Campling 1981;
Williams and Schoultz 1982; Grewal et al. 1988; Barron 1990; Millett 1991;
Sutcliffe and Symons 1993) is part of a growing recognition of the inevitably
political nature of social research.

Research tends to be owned and controlled by researchers, or by those who,
in turn, own and control the researchers. Those who remain powerless to
influence the processes of information gathering, the identification of truth,
and the dissemination of findings are usually the subjects of the research,
those very people whose interests the research may purport to serve.

In the context of vulnerable groups who are likely to be in receipt of human
services, this absence of ownership or control is likely to be particularly
marked. Disabled people have begun to voice strongly their concern that research done in their name may still fail utterly to take account of their view of
the world. As women did, they too have begun to articulate their own experiences of disability and the frameworks of thinking and research questions
which arise from those experiences:

> Agenda setting, whether it be in policies, policy making or service provi-
> sion, is part of a process of struggle and this is equally true of agenda
> setting in disability research . . . the major issue for the 1990s should be:
> do researchers wish to join with disabled people and use their expertise
> and skills in their struggles against oppression, or do they wish to con-
> tinue to use these skills and expertise in ways which disabled people find
> oppressive?

(Oliver 1990)

The issues are, as Oliver suggests, political. They are about controlling the
development of knowledge and understanding – about ownership.

As a student I chose psychology, with sociology and philosophy thrown in. This was perhaps not a surprising choice, (although I have never been clear where the decision came from), and helped me to explore, although not resolve, those key concerns. Sociology provided fascinating accounts of the mechanisms of inequality in society, philosophy offered Gilbert Ryle and *The Concept of Mind* (Ryle 1949) with an exposition on how realities and meanings are indeed constructed rather than absolute, and psychology offered the hope of tools with which to go forth and . . . and what?

I doubted the relevance of professional knowledge to real problems. My professional training with Doctors John and Elizabeth Newson at Nottingham University taught me to respect and learn from the craft skills and insights of parents, and working in the disability field as a psychologist with parent groups and families showed me an urgent agenda of issues and practical concerns of which many professionals, and certainly much academic teaching, seemed blissfully unaware. I tried to understand and to respond and learned a great deal in the process.

Shared action research[2]

Twenty-five years on from graduating, I have now spent half of that time at the Open University, having moved from professional to academic life. I have kept up my interest and work in the disability area, with an emphasis on shifting the power back from professionals to disabled people. A specific impetus for this recent shared approach to research arose from belonging to the Learning Disability Research Group described in the Introduction. This group had an emerging focus on participative research and grew eventually into the Reflective Research Group responsible for this book. I had drafted a paper on what I thought participative research meant. In framing some ideas within that paper, I suggested that control over the formulation of the research questions themselves was a key factor in determining who really owned the research.

The project described here was a chance for me to take up my own challenge and see whether sharing the development of the actual research agenda, the nature of questions to be addressed, could be achieved working with a group of people with learning disabilities. A simpler explanation altogether is that I chose this project because I thought it would be fun. I enjoyed the contact I had, from an academic base, with local services and service users and felt that I would have at least some of the necessary skills to make such an undertaking work. Moreover, having failed to get funding at that stage for a full research project, this offered at least an enjoyable starting point, manageable in the time I had available.

It also fitted in well with the much longer term interest I had in developing and evaluating Shared Action Planning as a service system. In this sense, the project was part of a larger action research project, which had started with the design, publication and fairly extensive implementation of Shared Action Planning. The notion of sharing the planning of the research agenda with an advisory group of service users, who might themselves be using the service system, appealed, therefore, as being thoroughly in keeping with the principles and practice of the overall approach. Perhaps this was Shared Action Research.[2]

An inspirational book, *Making Sense Together: An Introduction to Wild Sociology* (O'Neill 1975), argues for such a shared approach at the level of a shared humanity and a shared exploration of life itself. He is quoted at the beginning of this chapter. The quote ends: 'To begin is confidently part of the work of building and sharing an understanding. It is ideally the institution of making sense together within a common life and a common world' (O'Neill 1975: 1). To embark on a journey of discovery, seeking some greater understanding, is, he suggests, something we do as ambassadors or representatives; 'or else by what right do we leave home and friends . . . and wander into regions where our own language and customs become self-conscious, strained and perhaps unusable?' To begin research with people is:

> to solicit an encounter between ourselves and others present to us here and now, or through their work and its legacy. Such a beginning is of the order of intimacy and revelation in which we discover a primitive sense of closeness. Yet our approach would be unbearable if it were not like the meeting of eyes in which there can be no primacy of the self but only a kind of alternating life. Our approach is rather an invitation to friendship and love, unsure yet certain. It is a warm embrace in which we are caught up in that overlap in which we spend our lives together and which invites comparison and understanding as much as fear and uncertainty. This is the ground for starting with one another.
>
> (O'Neill 1975: 4–5)

Such an account, presenting research in effect as an existential pursuit, seems rather grand as a framework for discussing this small-scale study. And yet, for me, it feels profoundly helpful. It presents honestly and boldly the importance of attending to the fundamental human relations involved. By what right should I study another, standing back, detached, objective, unless I do it in the name of friendship – unless it is 'the work of knowledge . . . only to open paths that others can follow'. The legitimation is there hand-in-hand with the shared recognition of uncertainty.

Sharing with the advisory group

What, then, was the reality of attempting to put some of these rather high flown ideas into practice. A number of issues troubled me:

1 Any claim to have set in motion a shared exploration of agendas and potential research questions is immediately challenged by the extent to which the focus of the research, an evaluation of Shared Action Planning, was already pre-determined, and by the fact that the whole process was instigated by me to assist me in my research. Could it ever then be seen as sharing?

2 My role in the research was itself complicated, given my own vested interest in the Shared Action Planning Process. This could only be seen as a part of

an ongoing action research process, particularly given my active previous involvement in, not only the development, but also the implementation of the process.

3 The applied and strategic nature of the research, in the sense that it is entwined with a process of training and implementation of a method of service delivery, makes boundaries almost impossible to maintain. Many individuals in the group became rapidly interested in either progressing or initiating their own Shared Action Planning, or in spreading the word to other service users, staff and parents. Holding on to my original intention of developing a research agenda became difficult and confusing.

Issues like these, and many others, were prevalent throughout, and I spent much of my time feeling completely bewildered about what was happening and whether I was doing anything useful or even sensible. I resorted frequently to the comforting thought that letting go of control involves risk and uncertainty, and feelings of confusion must therefore be expected. Working with a group of people with learning difficulties, the feelings of mutual uncertainty were considerable. A gradual building of shared understanding and a sense of shared enterprise emerged, although issues of responsibility and leadership remained problematic.

The process was overtly designed to nurture, clarify and develop the implicit research questions of this group of people – to give them control, albeit within the limits of a framework defined by me. The experience did not really feel much like that. To put it another way, if that was happening, and it possibly was, it was incredibly hard to detect and hang on to it given all the other things that were happening too. Perhaps the other, hidden, purpose of the exercise was that of seeking legitimation for my endeavours, seeking to create a relationship within which paths could be opened and a basis for sharing with one another could be achieved. Perhaps I was seeking permission and authenticity as their ambassador or representative in furthering the research, rather like Fiona Williams' notion of a 'minute taker', there simply to record and represent others' views.

All my attempts to describe the experience to date have sounded far more like an account of those aspects of the sharing process, that is, a description of a developing relationship and shared understanding, than like an account of discovering the group's implicit research agenda. The process dominated the purpose. To convey something of what went on in the course of the meetings, they are described below under four headings:

Creating a Forum
Assumptions and Expectations
Communication Processes
A Shared Enterprise.

Creating a forum

Sharing cannot happen quickly, and relaxed group meetings seemed the best format. Practicalities of organization were real. The need, for example, to arrange lifts, check timetables, avoid too much disruption of people's schedules, ensure that day centre workers were informed when necessary (it was not always easy to work out – whose responsibility this should be? Mine? Theirs? The social worker's?), arrange coffee and tea, send reminder letters and so on. Having a helpful and positive social worker taking part made it possible. I really doubt if I could have managed otherwise.

Looking back over the meetings, important aspects of the forum we created together seemed to include things like time, trust, comfort, enjoyment, and tolerance of uncertainty. The group created its own ice-breaker over coffee at the first meeting with a good five minute animated conversation about football before we began to talk about Shared Action Planning and people making choices about their lives. The ensuing discussion to which everyone contributed some account of themselves took most of the rest of the session. Setting another date took 20 minutes and provided an opportunity for individuals to think through their commitments, whether they wanted to come again (they did), and when they could manage. It felt as if the process was working, but very slowly.

Assumptions and expectations

Everyone comes with his or her own set of assumptions and expectations as to what the meetings will be like. Mine in particular may differ from theirs. They are likely to have particular and different strengths, in terms of relevant personal experiences and knowledge. Becoming sensitive to and aware of those starting points (including my own) is a crucial task.

Unless a group has met only to socialize over coffee, there has to be an agenda of some kind, however informal. We agreed on one at the outset, in the sense that I suggested one and they agreed, and I then took responsibility for deciding on a focus each week. I felt, however, continually torn between this controlling role and my wish to be as open and receptive as possible. Discussing records, and the issue of access, for example, involves me in lengthy explanation and then leaves me confused when the conversation is diverted unexpectedly (group participants names have been changed apart from my own):

> *Ann:*　So there might be records kept about you and sometimes you don't know what's in them. People might write things down about you and keep them and it's difficult for you to know what's in them if you can't read and people don't say to you, 'Here are your records'. They put them in a filing cabinet.
>
> *Stephen:*　Would they keep the records if a person leaves the place – or what?
>
> *Ann:*　Yes, like you said you moved from x to y. Probably they would have sent your records with you when you went.
>
> *Stephen:*　Um I don't think . . . I haven't got . . . the only thing I brought was I think some class photographs.

Mary:	(Social worker) The thing is about records though sometimes you don't know they're there.
Mark:	A record um – is always there. If you want to do something very silly would that er would a record?
Ann:	You mean if you got in trouble would they write that down.
Mark:	If the police have er a complaint they could tell (names two social workers).
Ann:	Sometimes people don't like that. They feel like – that happened when I was fifteen or whatever – it's not fair.
Mark:	That is fair.
Douglas:	They might say 'I'm not going near him. He's dangerous.' You see things on telly, like this man who murdered a 9-year-old child. Well I think he should be kept there – life imprisonment should mean that, till he's dead. I'm sorry, but I've got strong views on that. That's where hanging should be compulsory.
Mark:	And they should bring the gallows back in Ireland.

What line should I take when the conversation turns suddenly to hanging, or when someone says, 'I think we should talk about Christmas today'? It is more complex than simply trying to keep a meeting on track, because there may be important messages for me to pick up – like, 'Perhaps you could help us set up a "Bring back hanging" campaign', or 'What you are saying is really boring', or, 'I don't know what you are talking about and this feels much more familiar', or simply, 'My preference is to talk about football'. As the whole point of the research process, and the focus of the research, is on people making their own choices and decisions, prioritizing my own agenda was a particularly acute dilemma.

What tended to happen was that the conversation would then take off, perhaps dominated by two or three people, until I tried, feeling very bossy, to bring it back onto track (that is, onto my track). I had to consider whether it was part of my role to teach people how to take part appropriately in a meeting of that kind or whether it was evading the issue to predefine some contributions as inappropriate? Could I be a teacher and an open-minded observer at the same time? I suspect I fulfilled their expectations by behaving in this rather controlling way, despite my own concerns. The trouble was that all this conflicted with my desire to find out what their agenda might be. When I tried to ask, it was often as if my questions fell into a void.

Communication processes

With the best will in the world, most of the issues I wanted to talk about with the group were abstract. The umbrella concept of Shared Action Planning was familiar to some people because they had been using it. Others wondered if perhaps it meant 'sharing a flat'.

Discussing 'what people want to do in their lives' as an approach, in the sense of 'Does this seem to you to be a good approach to use?' is bewildering in the extreme, as is the idea of having access or control of your own records. With one or two exceptions, people were totally baffled by my inept attempts to explain what I wanted us to talk about. On a tape recording of an early session, I bumble on with the silence of confusion quite tangible in the background. When someone offers a helping hand with the comment, 'Yes, records, we have a record player in our flat', it is clear that things are not going well.

Communication was enormously helped as we built a shared set of reference points using examples which were meaningful within the group. This took time, of course, but the discussion of record-keeping, before it wandered into other realms, was built upon a personalized vocabulary. Records were 'like Jane's life history book; like the drawings Martin did to remind us what we talked about; like your social worker might write down to remember what you did'.

Unexpected contributions seemed to form part of the negotiation over what we really might be talking about. People had interesting stories to tell which seemed tangential at the time, but somehow in the end played a key part in helping the group to develop a sense of identity. We got to know each other and extended our shared vocabulary and reference points through these spontaneous stories which emerged from time to time.

At other times the answers or comments seemed unexpected because they were not what I was hoping to hear. An example of this was my first attempt to open up a very central area of discussion by asking about the different ways in which they felt staff could be helpful. (Helpful relationships is a core concept in Shared Action Planning.) I had anticipated that people might want staff to take an advocacy role on their behalf, to act as trouble shooters, and to be good listeners. Instead the main emphasis in all the initial responses was the one I had been hoping to move away from: 'Staff can help us to learn. You need to learn to do things. Learn to hoover the floor.'

In a sense this was reassuring, as it seemed at least to demonstrate that I could not lead or influence the group to give me the answers I wanted to hear. In fact, in the end, they produced a rich and wide-ranging set of commentaries which continued to emerge throughout the sessions (see, for example the quotes from the video below), and included all I had hoped for and more.

Despite such difficulties, we seemed to make progress as a group. We got much better at communication as time went on. We drew flip-chart pictures to act as minutes or a reminder of our discussions; I produced an illustrated summary of the discussions; we took some photographs and wrote an account of our meetings for a local newsletter. We began to develop a shared history and memories of fun things we had tried, like role play games of helpful and unhelpful ways of listening or teaching. All those gradual developments made it so much easier to talk together in a relaxed way.

At first it seemed difficult to know how to apply any previous knowledge and skill in this new situation. It was as if I felt that in trying to suspend any judgement or expectations, I must also suspend any certainty about what my role should be. The result was rather a vacuum which I filled from time to time by tending to play the role of group leader. Not to do so felt like putting the group on the spot, and it was a difficult balance to try to achieve.

I recognized in this an indication that I saw it as my responsibility to ensure that individuals felt comfortable in the situation and that their contributions were being valued. The experience, therefore, of being met with baffled looks, yawns, falling asleep or embarrassed, baffled agreement, was quite unnerving. Evaluating one's performance in this context was certainly daunting. Retrospectively it appears to be a catch-22 situation. To have performed confidently and smoothly as an effective group leader would have been a mistake; but performing rather hesitantly in an uncertain and ill-defined role felt inevitably rather unsatisfactory too. Both Pam Shakespeare's and Dorothy Atkinson's chapters describe similar quandaries in conducting conversations with older people.

A shared enterprise

Over time everyone began to greet me and each other as friends – not just in a friendly way, which they had always done, but really as friends. The atmosphere of the meetings changed. There emerged a sense of togetherness about the group. I still would tend to lead it, perhaps more so, but in a much more facilitative way which helped them to be more in control. I began to feel more in tune with their wishes, ideas and feelings; in short, to get to know them.

Relationships between group members developed; teasing became a feature. A young woman, who was reduced to embarrassed silence by her crush on a young man in the group, became able to tease him happily. Looking at a photograph of group members where he featured centrally, she glanced across at him and said loudly, 'Who is that person in the middle?'

As the group relaxed and took charge of itself, my control diminished. Suddenly the group had decided we should make a video about our work together to be followed by a conference. I was not sure if I had the time. Fortunately the Social Services Department via the training department later took up the notion of a conference and worked with members of the group to expedite that. They successfully ran an all-day conference for about 50 service-users with learning disabilities (staff were not allowed to take part) to which I was invited to contribute.

In the meantime we had moved ahead with the video idea. The group decided how to approach it and what should be included. The sense of a shared enterprise took any remaining pressure off and the filming went really well. People said things on camera which brought out key points. Martin, for example, told us that he did not feel comfortable about asking to see his records in the filing cabinet in the office because, 'They think you're being nosey'. Douglas talked vehemently about how some people can 'make you feel two feet tall'. We heard about how parents can 'send you to bed without supper – being punished like that – it's not helpful'.

Suzanne, who has great difficulty talking and can only speak painfully slowly, told me quietly afterwards that she felt the group had really helped her to have the confidence to speak out more. On video, she said, 'It's helpful if people can give you confidence.' Asked how people can do that, she said 'They can give you confidence if they have confidence in you'.

Given that this was a group who had met only half a dozen times, the quality and confidence of their contributions was a tribute to their perceptiveness. It took time and the development of comfortable relationships for the comments to emerge, but with that they were keen to express their views.

There comes a point when the successful development of such strong working relations presents another kind of risk. No longer the risk of failure, but the risk of over-commitment and expectations that cannot be met. With minimal real time available, what is the appropriate way to control the power of the relationships that have developed. The group wanted to go on meeting. Apart from completing the video, showing it with them, and helping with the conference, I have run out of time and we have not met again recently.

A research agenda!

In some ways looking for the bit of the process that was about identifying research questions feels, in the midst of these rather powerful concerns, like looking for a needle in a haystack. Yet there were answers in there. The discussions about helpfulness, for example, provided a clear set of criteria which could be used to evaluate Shared Action Planning from the service-users' perspective.

Does Shared Action Planning promote or support or encourage helpfulness in the form of:

listening and understanding
giving people time
giving people confidence
others having confidence in you
helping you to do things
finding alternative ways to achieve something
not making you feel small
showing you how to do things
helping you to learn
not deciding things for you
not punishing you
listening to what you want in your life?

A research proposal is the next step, designed to address that question (and others which featured, relating to record-keeping and life choices). The group could be invited to have a continuing role as a research advisory group. This would be the formal account of the project.

The memorable aspects of the experience, however, were the processes involved which felt much more obvious, and more preoccupying than the overt purpose:

1 Opening up channels of communication – learning how better to be understood and to understand.
2 Developing relationships and group identity.

3 Discovering ways of sharing meanings and feelings.
4 Identifying progress and recording it for ourselves and for others.
5 Undertaking a shared enterprise.

In O'Neill's terms we found a way of starting out together, and that was what seemed to matter most. It felt like a move towards 'making sense together within a common life and a common world'. It provided legitimation for further research and the sense of bestowing on me the right to act as ambassador or representative. It felt, in fact, like a good beginning.

Notes

1. Shared Action Planning is an approach to working with people with learning disabilities, designed to encourage empowering relationships with staff, in which people are increasingly enabled to make their own choices and decisions (Brechin and Swain 1987).
2. For the notion that this might be described as shared action research, I am indebted to Joanna Bornat who made the suggestion after reading a draft of this paper. The concept of action research is well established with reference to situations where development and evaluation proceed hand in hand, each feeding into the other.

7

Presenting

Joanna Bornat

Kids. The room is crawling with little Barnard girls and their tape re-
corders, pestering people for 'oral history'. A pair camp by Mrs Axelrod,
clicking on whenever she starts awake and mutters some Yiddish. Sophie,
who speaks, says she's raving about the harness-eyes breaking and
shackles bouncing on the floor, some shirt-factory tangle in her mind.
Gems, they think they're getting, oral history gems.

There are starting to be Rebeccas again, the little Barnard girls, and
Sarahs and Esthers, after decades of Carol, Sally and Debbie. The one who
tapes me is a Raisele, which was my mother's name.

'We're trying to preserve it', she says with a sweet smile for an old man.

'What, Yiddish? I don't speak.'

'No', she says. 'Anarchism. The memories of anarchism. Now that it's
served its dialectical purpose.'

'You're a determinist.'

She gives me a look. They think we never opened a book. I don't tell
her I've written a few, it wouldn't make an impression. If it isn't on tape
or film it doesn't register. Put my name in the computer, you'll draw a
blank.

'Raisele,' I say. 'That's a pretty name.'

'I learned it from an exchange student. I used to be Jody.'

(Sayles 1992: 27)

I first began interviewing as an oral historian in 1975. By chance I happened to
be reading the short story 'At the anarchists' convention', published in 1975,
when I was writing this chapter. As I read it I realized that I wouldn't have been
able to cope with John Sayles' account of an oral history exchange when it was

first published. His cynical and jokey style raises issues which I wasn't prepared to confront then. I have changed.

It is perhaps the skill of a writer and film maker like John Sayles which enabled him to see more of the dynamics of interviewing than I, a serious and politically committed researcher into facts and truths, was unable to acknowledge when I set out to be an oral historian. He identifies the older person as an active and aware protagonist in the interview. So Leo Gold, who is his narrator, describes generational distance, when he talks about the 'Barnard girls', a 'sweet smile' and fashions in first names. He hints at a multiplicity of accounts, with his reference to 'oral history gems' and the personal history he hides from Raisele. He gives a sense of technological and social estrangement when he mentions tape, film, the computer and her brief acquittal of anarchism. He is suggesting a contradiction between Raisele's commitment to preserve a past and his own very much living and continuing resistance. And he suspects that his interviewee isn't exactly who she presents herself to be. She's a 'Jody' not a 'Raisele', or at least that's what she says she used to be. And then there is the dilemma of what to do about Mrs Axelrod's account. She is presented as someone who is 'raving' but she is clearly communicating some part of her identity. We never find out how the interview goes because the story ends with the old anarchists beginning to barricade themselves into the hotel suite they booked for their convention. With Leo's strong reservations about the whole oral history enterprise this looks like a more satisfying outcome for him at least.

Back in 1975, I found the process of interviewing older people about their own life histories overwhelmingly humbling. I felt that I had been given a charge, a political task, to reveal a past that had been concealed by a powerful class-ridden tradition of history making. And I was convinced that making a hidden oral history public meant making changes both for the public record and for anyone who identified with these hitherto hidden accounts. I don't think I realized how much it could also change me.

The interviews I have been involved in over the last 17 years or so have each left different impressions on me. Sometimes it has taken a while for implications to set in. At other times I have been taken aback during the interview itself. In this chapter I look at the interview as a way of presenting ourselves to others. I look at presenting a life course – how we each see each other in time; presenting an identity – how we display ourselves now; and presenting a purpose – the extent to which both sides declare what each wants from the interview.

Seventeen years ago I was less concerned with the perspective of the interviewee. In this chapter I draw on my experience as someone who has continued to interview 'for history' but who has increasingly found myself interviewing with social welfare issues in mind. As an oral historian I am an investigator of the past through memory and individual witness. I became a lecturer in health and social welfare with a special interest in gerontology. This means that I find myself in the role of investigator of the significance of the past for present individual and collective experience. Looking back over interviews which I have carried out at various points during the last 17 years, I find that I'm more aware these days that the interview is a product of a shaping which both sides are involved in – interviewee and interviewer. I've moved from feeling that as an oral historian I am the liberator of a story which can contribute to understandings of social and political change to an understanding that I am listening for accounts which relate to present circumstances and conditions and which suggest awareness and significance for the interviewee. So, from a conviction that I was helping an older person to reclaim ground, establish an identity and value in society – creating a product – I have moved to a point where I am listening to the older person actively shaping that telling – and I'm learning from the process.

Oral history, with few exceptions (Seldon and Papworth 1983), has mainly been working-people's history. It provides a hearing for versions of history which tend to go un-noticed by historians who focus on documentary evidence. To talk to people about working lives, domestic relationships, childhood, experiences of migration, racism, exclusions, free time and pleasures is to challenge historical and political orthodoxies. But it is also more than that, like other oral historians, I saw the interview as a source of data which was untarnished and more real than any other type of data I had previously sought out. Following Paul Thompson, my supervisor of a slowly developing thesis, I agreed that: 'Oral evidence, by transforming the "objects" of study into "subjects", makes for a history which is not just richer, more vivid and heartrending, but *truer*' (his emphasis) (Thompson 1978: 90).

In changing my understanding of what interviewing means I have not been alone. Other oral historians have developed more interpretative understandings of their role as interviewers. In the second edition of *The Voice of the Past*, Paul Thompson devotes a whole chapter to 'Memory and the Self' (1988). Ron Grele, a US oral historian writes:

> we look at oral history as a historiographic act and . . . we examine the structure and use of history as articulated in the interview. Most importantly, this view gives proper respect to those we interview. It assumes that they are capable of complex cultural formulations, that they can interpret their own pasts, that they can look at themselves and us critically. It also assumes that they can and do use history, and that they can use it to actively involve themselves in the cultural dialogue in a fully participatory manner. People become not simply objects of study but part of the community of discourse.
>
> (Grele 1991: 271–2)

And Luisa Passerini, writing in Italy, argues of:

> the impossibility of making direct use of oral memories as immediately revealing facts and events. Rather, they reveal a tension between forms of behaviour and mental representations expressed through particular narrative guises.
>
> (Passerini 1989: 194)

Meanwhile, ethnographers were debating their own involvement in the process of data collection. In particular James Clifford began to question the rights of the ethnographer to interpretative distance and argued for a more collaborative and reflexive approach between academic researchers and their subjects (Pearce and Chen 1989; Stacey 1991).

Ethnographers and oral historians still have their particular kinds of interest and enquiry; my own understanding is one that has been shaped by an involvement in the concerns, perspectives and welfare of older people. Seventeen years on from my first interviews I am no less humbled, no less struck by the power of authenticity in the spoken word, no less aware of the process of interviewing as change-invoking. But during the succeeding years things have happened to me, personal, political, academic, that have led me to a different understanding of the meaning of interviewing both for me and for people I interview. When I talk to oral historians now about the craft, I usually point out to them that their practice takes them into new territory, the world of older people. What I tell them is what I discovered myself as I became more aware of issues in gerontology and began to listen to the person and make the links between the personal and social politics of welfare with the class and social politics of history.

Presenting a life course

It is more or less a convention in oral history interviewing that we structure our questions around the familiar chronology of the life course. It is certainly a convenience to be able to start at a notional beginning point, childhood, and then to go on through the decades of life, first job, courting, marriage, children and the middle years of life. It is a convention which from the beginning I tended to assume my interviewee would recognize and be instantly in tune with. I present a norm, an assumption of a simple straightforward progression. In my early interviews this never seemed to be a problem, I heard a straightforward chronology emerge and was happy to be able to fill out the life stages in my data analysis sheets for each person. Now I can see that sometimes the chronology is more obvious to me than the person I am interviewing:

'The way to begin is by asking you to say what your name is and when you were born.'
'Do you want to have my name when I was born, or now?'
'If you like, yes'

Looking back at the transcript of that interview I can see how inadequate my response was. I equivocated in my answer when I could perhaps have pursued a line which could have opened up an exploration of changing names and what that means. I could have deserted my life-course trajectory and focused on an issue instead. But I didn't, I stuck to my familiar and safe progress through life. Joan is someone I interviewed quite recently in connection with a collection of essays about older women (Bernard and Meade 1993). She had not been certain about how to present her life to me. She told me she had not put it all together before. I had assumed she had a life-course perspective to present to me. Instead, I almost had to prise it out of her. At the end of her interview she surprised me:

'All right then, shall I switch it off?'
'Yes, unless you've got anything else'
'I don't know, always afterwards I always think of things I'd like to ask someone and I'm impatient with myself for having – '
'I think marvellous how you've balanced questions and letting me ramble on.'
'Well I didn't feel you were rambling on at all'
'Didn't you?'
'No'
'Oh good. I felt I was at times.'
'No, I felt – '
'Done me a power of good I can tell you!'
'Really?'
'Yes'
'Oh, that's very nice to hear'
'I've never done this, it's a long time'

I had assumed that Joan's memories fell neatly into a chronological life course and that she would present them to me in that form. In the interview I encountered first uncertainty and then, finally, a recognition and a positive evaluation from her of what I had presented as an ordering. She found that she enjoyed making connections between the stages of her life. Perhaps she was enjoying the feeling of making her life what Grele calls 'anthropologically strange' to herself (Grele 1991). Joan lives very much in the present and connects with contemporary issues. Born in 1913 into a wealthy landowning family she described a life that has not followed conventional patterns. When their children were small just after the Second World War she and her husband lived in a commune, later she divorced and later still she became active in peace politics. We were able to reach some form of compromise over my preference for a life-course structure mainly because Joan's life had followed certain social and biological stages. She married, she had children. She seemed pleased to have had an opportunity to review her life in a connected thread but I felt I had pressed a narrative form on her.

I interviewed Ray for the same project. Ray is a single woman and, in asking her to set out her life story, I began to realize that my simple milestoning chronology was unhelpful for both of us. Indeed she resisted my attempts to explore the conventional staging post of marriage. The result is that she seemed to move quickly over the middle years of her life:

And I've always had quite a lot of friends of both sexes. But then there came a period when I wasn't well, I used to faint a lot and one thing and another. And then I'd all this stomach trouble and things. And then eventually they found out I'd gallstones and whatnot. And then I was in hospital. And then when I came out, when I'd sort of recovered sufficiently, I mean, my parents you know, had to look after them. My life sort of tailed off a bit . . . I've always been single, and I don't, I wouldn't – if I'd been younger I could have got married actually, I've had a few proposals.

> But I can't get married just for the sake of being married status. I mean, I couldn't marry anybody you know.

Ray's family commitments remained her family of origin. She and her, also unmarried, sister became carers of relatives, but Ray combined these roles with full-time paid work. It was later, when she talked about her paid work that she became most animated, describing different jobs as ward orderly, book-keeper and an attempt to get an outdoor job as a meter reader. Ray's life course switched between different systems of milestoning. Paid work provided a certain continuity, though without a sense of culmination since she saw her best years financially as being in her 20s and early 30s. Unpaid caring work arrived late in her life when her mother became housebound. As I interviewed her, I gradually became aware of the way the middle years of her life might have gone unremarked, if I had stuck to questions around her single status. In fact in the end she turned me off that track deliberately:

> You do meet people that you think you could spend your life with. But it turned out it's not worked out, and people die on you and things like that. I don't say any more about that. So that was that. But I've not regretted really being single. I suppose if I, I suppose in a way, I often think, well I haven't done anything with my life, but I think if you're needed by whoever, your life's not wasted.

Looking back through the transcript I get a sense of a private life course of relationships which she did not choose to reveal. The conventionally milestoned life course invites a logging of only those public confirmations of life events, marriage being the obvious one. Ray presents her life in a series of intertwining life courses in caring, work and leisure activities (Allen 1989). It was only afterwards, reading through the transcript of her interview that I became aware of this. In the interview I invited her to present a chronology which highlighted a narrative which she felt unable or unwilling to complete. She resisted this with her own timeline of life events.

I have used these two examples to show how imposing a chronology can work well for some people, but not for others. I have learned to value these differences. What I see and hear now is a variability in the way life events are presented. When I first set out as an oral historian it was a homogeneity that I wanted to hear. Interviewing for history I wanted to discover confirmation of my suppositions and research questions. Interviewing with social welfare issues in mind I prefer to hear the diversity which provokes me into identifying new meanings and new connections.

The result is that, when I interview for oral history now, I find that I want to know more about the whole person through different life stages. I think I am more tolerant of diversions from my train of questioning and perhaps less thrown when an interviewee like Ray chooses their own chronology of events or main preoccupations. Thinking about Joan's interview, I am now more aware of differences in understanding about a life. I feel I cannot make assumptions about how people will react to the formula for unravelling an oral history that I present them with.

Presenting an identity

Looking for someone to interview usually means making choices based on identities which I define and then look for. My first set of oral history interviews in 1975 grew out of letters to local newspapers in the Colne Valley area of West Yorkshire. I described the kind of experience I wanted to hear about and several older women contacted me, almost as identikit versions of what I was looking for. I wanted to interview women with memories of working in the wool textile industry around the period of the First World War. They presented me with the right identities.

The identity I presented was someone who was doing research for a thesis at university. I was in my early 30s, married, and the mother of two young children. I also by now lived in the south of England, though I was always careful to point out that I was really a northerner. A researcher with northern connections was how I wanted to be seen by them. I didn't say that I was a disenchanted sociologist who, as a committed communist, had a bad experience being taught by structural functionalists in the 1960s, and who consequently had turned to labour history, trying to make my academic work fit with my personal political convictions. I could also have said that I was never too certain about my own academic credibility. Oral history provided me with a legitimate position on the margins of academe. Doing oral history was beginning to become a way of making historical research a piece of political action. It seemed to promise a way of bringing together different parts of my life.

I was a younger, middle-class woman interviewing older working-class women about a part of their life from which in many cases they had almost disconnected. With few exceptions it seemed that my interviewees had almost set on one side their early mill years. Most had left the mill on marrying, at the end of the First World War, and though many went back as their children grew up, somehow those early years had become separated off. Interviewing them about their early days as 13- and 14-year-old millworkers meant legitimizing a part of their lives which had become distanced. Their identities as young women and girls began to emerge. I felt that they enjoyed the retrieval of those years. There was a turning point one day in a sheltered flat in Slaithwaite when, after I thanked someone for her interview, she responded by thanking me. Until then I simply had not considered that this process of interviewing could be one from which we both got something.

It was this retrieval of past identities at a point in life when older women may sense a closing in of opportunities for self-expression and individuality which I have since realized my interviewees were responding so positively to (Grele 1991: 226). There were particular memories about becoming a worker – bringing home your wage to give to your mother, playing about with the other young workers, changing jobs to get more experience, taking on an adult role:

'Can you remember the day you took home your first wage?'
'Well you think you know a thing then you see, don't you? But you got a penny in the shilling, it was six shillings we got as first wage. I remember now and you got a penny in the shilling spending money . . . and then

when our boys went – and of course I was a weaver then and I took me
wage home and . . . when they'd gone soldiering and I know I used to give
me mother me spending money back because she hadn't so much to go
on with.'

(Miss Eva Varley interviewed 8 July 1975)

Later, I became much more involved in the movement which validated
reminiscence as a way of working with older people. I became aware of how
important the presentation of different past identities is to older people
(Adams 1984; Coleman 1986; Norris 1986; Bornat 1989). Looking back now, I
think it had a special significance for these older women. They recalled identities which they were able to present as evidence of themselves as lively, active
and productive young women (Personal Narratives Group 1989: 11). When I
came to write up my thesis, I questioned the extent to which participation in
the labour market gave them autonomy (Bornat 1978; Bornat 1980). My interpretation as an oral historian drawing on interviews and documents identified
lives of young women which were ultimately constrained by structural ine-
qualities in the home and workplace.

Nevertheless, in the process of interviewing and the choices these older
millworkers made about presenting their lives, I now see that recall of their
early identities was both an attempt to meet my needs as a researcher and a
gratifying experience which they were maximizing for themselves in old age. I
learned about their life experiences, and as I did I found myself reframing my
perspective of these older women. Their present identities, as retired, sometimes frail and disabled older women, reformed as they revealed their past
experience, knowledge and skills in answers to my questions.

My recognition of the significance of earlier identities is only part of the
process. Recently I have come to recognize that handing back the transcript for
the interviewee to complete a chosen identity is an essential step. In my early
stages of being an oral historian, the 'moment' of the interview was then all
important for me, rather like the discovery of a new document. Revisions were
unthinkable simply because the oral account was so 'true'. But getting more
drawn into the interview as an exchange and as having meanings beyond the
'moment', has made me question that freezing and encapsulating process. The
Jewish Women in London Group argues for giving back on the grounds that this
allows interviewees to have authorship and interpretation rights rather than
'groups of academic and political onlookers' (Jewish Women in London 1989).

Katherine Borland describes an impasse with her own grandmother who
rejected her interpretation of her life history. She describes this as a particular
problem for feminists. What do you do when women disagree with your
understanding? After she represented her grandmother's life as a struggle for
female autonomy, her grandmother responded with a 14 page letter in dis-
agreement. Though her grandmother finally came to understand feminism,
this was as a postscript to the interview rather than a working through together (Borland 1991).

The move away from a purely oral history approach to interviewing has left
me with something which is almost a block in terms of rights to interpretation.

The closer I feel I am to the process – the social relationship of the interview – the less certainty I feel I can claim to interpret the product – the identities of the people I interview. This seems to be an almost unresolvable problem. My own move away from interpreting and towards a way of letting identities define themselves came in the interviews with Ray, Pat, Joan and others. When I came to interpretation, I deliberately minimized my own role in an attempt to foreground their voices. I chose not to include any secondary sources through literature references and comparative evaluations. I was interested to see how Judith Stacey dealt with the dilemma of the researcher's own involvement and detachment in her study of women in Silicon valley:

> I adopt a dual set of narrative strategies. In the ethnographic chapters I attempt to employ a self-reflexive voice. I am actively present as I was during my fieldwork – participating, interrogating, reacting, learning, interpreting, erring . . . In the ethnographic chapters I also severely curtail my use of the more abstract sociological voice . . . in the more analytical contextualizing chapters . . . I risk the less reflexive, realist voice of the conventional, interpretive sociologist that I am now not willing, or able to disown.
>
> (Stacey 1990: 37)

In my own case I excerpted the interviews, linked them with the barest narrative I could achieve and handed the whole piece back to the five women I had interviewed. Most of the changes I was asked to make were brief and factual, but there were two which I was forced to come to terms with.

Charanjit asked me to change her speech into a form which she felt would be more English. This was an issue I had confronted once before with someone who rewrote his transcribed speech, neatly removing all trace of his distinctive Jewish East End speech. I conceded regretfully. I was forced to do so again. My understanding of the representation of her identity was that readers would appreciate and engage with Charanjit more readily if they read her as she sounded. I could hear her voice as I read her words. But her preference was otherwise. She described herself in India as being an educated woman. She had been a radio broadcaster in the early 1950s. In England, she and her husband enjoyed some standing in the Sikh community. He was a journalist and writer in Punjabi, their language. They had grown old as white-collar workers living in a council flat. Though I had represented some of the richness of their lives in the account I had stitched together, the form of the account I wanted to present conflicted with her own sense of identity. What she gained was control over her own presentation. What I felt I lost was a way of presenting through the medium of verbatim speech the dilemmas of her experience as an older Asian woman in Britain.

The second change I was asked to make was slight in terms of words but large in terms of my own personal and mental revisions. During three hours of interviewing Pat, I learned about her life as a top cycle wheel builder with a deserved reputation for skill in what is predominantly a man's trade. She told me she had been married twice, both brief experiences, one marriage ending in divorce early in her life, the other ending in death just after retirement. This identity I faithfully edited into the account. It presented some nice contrasts with the other four women, particularly with its focus on work and the independent life style.

Pat's late amendment therefore came as something as a surprise. She asked me to insert just a sentence to put the record straight. She 'had a son but now has no contact with him'. She wanted no other change to the account, no explanation in the text. So it stands, but with what I see as a vast understatement of her life story.

I think that as interpreters we have to settle for less than we had all hoped for whether interviewing for oral history or with social welfare in mind. Perhaps the kind of shared experience I want is unattainable, and we have to accept the differences in identity and status that are presented as a means to stepping back from a position of dominance as interviewers.

Presenting a purpose

> Both interpreters and narrators approach the process of creating a personal narrative with their own agendas. These . . . affect the shape and focus of the text.
>
> (Personal Narratives Group 1989: 202)

The original idea of my oral history interviews was that we both, the interviewee and I, shared one purpose – mine! This was not so self-seeking as it sounds. Presenting myself as an oral historian usually meant that I included some account of the way I felt my interviewee's words were going to subvert or replace the established historical record. I may not always have presented this directly as empowerment, but I increasingly came to see the process as just that.

My work as an oral historian led me directly into work with older people. In the early 1980s this was an easy step to take. I took a job with the education department of the charity Help the Aged and was among the group which successfully launched the first reminiscence pack for older people, *Recall*. I spent those years in an almost evangelistic state, finding eager audiences for the pack amongst paid and unpaid carers who found that their interest in listening to what frail and dependent older people wanted to talk to them about, their past experience, was at last being legitimized as good practice.

These experiences of 'giving a voice' were followed by work with community groups, when, in the mid 1980s I chaired Exploring Living Memory, a series of mass exhibitions of group and individual life histories held on London's South Bank and funded by the Greater London Council. Together the exhibits comprised a lively and participative representation and reclamation by London's different communities of past identities and experience, an alternative history for London (Bornat unpublished).

These events were showcases of collective purpose at a time when London's politics were unashamedly left populist and challenging of orthodoxies. Life histories still have a way of being political in the caring and fragmenting

1990s. As I listen to accounts of the past, the sheer heterogeneity of personal experience provides an essential support for the optimistic conviction that if things could be different then, well maybe they can be different again.

Such openly political purposes are relatively easy to share, if allegiances are declared and diversity is respected, yet some women ethnographers and oral historians have begun to look at this issue more self-critically. Rejecting essentialist assumptions about shared purpose and identities, they look to working in community contexts for a way of resolving dilemmas around the exploitation of women by feminist researchers (Gluck and Patai 1991). Unfortunately, and despite my experiences with Exploring Living Memory, I cannot see community as a safe alternative. Community has too many contradictory meanings to provide an adequate guarantee of democracy and shared purpose for women (Bornat 1992; Williams 1992c).

Have my own interviews shown me any way round this dilemma? I want to look at examples of collective and personal purpose as a way of exploring my own understanding. Looking back to a series of group interviews carried out over a year on a north London housing estate during 1986–7, when I worked for the adult education service of the Inner London Education Authority, I feel that I can now see how different voices joined in to give one account which was both publicly acceptable and collectively constructed. At one level this was the depiction of the history of a group of council tenants. At another level, it was the deliberate identification by a group of older men and women of values of heroism, communality and class allegiance in immediate post-war Britain in the face of loss of status as older council tenants in the mid-1980s (Woodberry Down Memories 1989). Though I could join in and identify with this purpose, there were many points at which I clearly had no shared experience, on grounds of age or class. I had to remain an outsider, though a valued one, as I am frequently assured.

I have also found out that purpose can be individual. One of my first interviewees in Colne Valley, I later recognized, had a clear purpose of her own. Her story was one of suffering and marginality she felt as a Quaker. She cried as she remembered her father's experience of rejection by her older stepbrothers and sisters, linking this to a passage in the *Messiah* she first heard when she was 11- or 12-years-old, 'and he was despised and rejected'. Now I might see her purpose as trying to communicate her depression to me, an outsider. Then I felt quite disempowered by her emotions. More recently, interviewing an older Chinese woman for a course on community care, about her own difficult early years in this country, I encountered the same need on the interviewee's part to communicate pain and suffering, partly as catharsis, partly as a means to inform through experience (Coleman 1993).

What I think I am beginning to learn, from the context in which I now work, where I use the past to help unravel or reveal present dilemmas, is a perspective which allows for the idea that older people may have a controlling role in the interview. Seen this way empowerment becomes less a question of freeing up the victims, the dispossessed, and more an issue of accepting that deliberate choices and decisions on the part of the interviewee may be shaping the content and direction of the interview. Where others talk of silences

(Passerini 1990) or 'uchronic' dreams of events that never happened (Portelli 1988) I think I see resistance and will. Though I still see the interview as a power relationship, I think I can see different expressions of power and purpose on both sides. I think I am now more prepared for the grit and determination which the other person is mediating and less inclined to think only in terms of disempowered victims. Though I am no less wary of creating an exploitative relationship, by 'mining' someone's past, I now see evidence of conscious collusion with the outcome in some cases, and positive enjoyment in participation in others.

Seventeen years after I first started interviewing, and as many years older, it may be that I am beginning to identify with the people I interview simply through the direct experience of becoming older myself. I share more life experiences with them than I did before. My children have grown up. I find myself spending more time talking about the needs of my older family members. Moreover, I have already been interviewed several times for my own experience as an oral historian. Of course, I am not suggesting that to develop some kind of insight into being on the other side of the microphone you have to become an older person. There are some practical experiences which I now see as essential preparation for arriving at some form of acceptable compromise at the end of the interview. Being interviewed oneself provides insights into the whole process; searching for answers to questions that do not quite fit your experience; hearing your own voice speak your thoughts out loud; being surprised at what you hear yourself say; worrying about pausing for too long in your answers and wondering what will happen to the tape afterwards.

Looking back, trying to bring the two parts of my experience together, still leaves me with dilemmas, though dilemmas which I feel I can see through a little more clearly. Dilemmas still attach to my status. As a lecturer with a professional commitment to research, I face the problem of differences in purpose and interpretation with most of my interviewees. However, I have remained someone who feels committed to enabling personal and political change. I still feel most at ease working with accounts where my interviewees and I share a common goal and work through the process of interpretation and editing together, but where I as an academic, an outsider on most occasions, declare my interests, explain my background and lay out what I feel are my skills.

It has been a slowly developing process of change for me. My understandings have been affected by interviews, projects and colleagues. What I hope I have learned, from interviewing with social welfare in mind, is to listen to the person behind the story, to accept conflicting and unexpected accounts, to take challenges to my authority as interviewer. But what I still want to keep from my experience of oral history interviewing is the broader context, the importance of validating and valuing a given individual life history and seeing it in relation to the greater scope of things.

8

Performing

Pam Shakespeare

I have recently been conducting a personal research project on the subject of the confused talk of people with dementing illnesses. Carrying out interviews with these people forced me to consider what, as a researcher, I bring of myself to fieldwork and how my own performance in the field contributes to the research I'm doing.

Ordinary everyday conversation is a sophisticated activity. We rarely consider its structure until we can't get a word in edgeways or we feel that we have been misunderstood. Conversation is what Donald Schön calls knowing-in-action (Schön 1990), a concept which embodies the knowledge people have to do things, a knowledge that doesn't always extend to being able to *explain* what they do. Everyone can converse rather well, as a general rule, although perhaps they would find conversational rules and structure difficult to articulate. Discovering how conversation is achieved is frequently brought about by being involved in it when it goes wrong. My research was partly based on recognition of this. Looking at the conversation of people who have been diagnosed as confused is to look at what Harold Garfinkel calls 'trouble' (Garfinkel 1967). However, a number of consequences usually follow from conversations going wrong. People often get embarrassed and upset. As a participant it is not easy to witness a *faux pas* without feeling sympathy for someone or wishing to do something about it. As a result, conversational participants usually work together to remedy what has gone wrong and to save face (Goffman 1976). What happens, though, when one of the participants is unable to contribute to the remedial work to keep the conversation going? I faced this situation several times in my fieldwork.

In my research I have talked to a number of people with confused speech, listened to some audio tapes of colleagues who had recorded conversations they had had with people with confused speech, and was lucky enough to receive an offer from one carer to record some talk with his wife in their home. This chapter concerns my own interviews. These were conducted mainly at an assessment clinic for psycho-geriatric illnesses, largely because I have no real entrée to the company of people with confused speech in my own social circle (although people with normal speech often made jokes about themselves being good subjects when they found out what my research was). After the consultant had done his assessment I would spend 20 minutes to half an hour talking to people with confused speech and to their carers who were invariably present. My hope was to have a relatively casual conversation with people individually, asking them questions such as where they came from, what they had done for a living and what their pastimes were. From there I intended to go on to transcribe and analyse the material mainly using conversational analysis. Would that life were so simple!

Before I began my interviews I hadn't anticipated the sense of embarrassment and responsibility I would feel in conducting the interviews. Early in my career I abandoned a PhD partly because I could never quite get away from the sense that ethnography is prying and because I found it stressful having to gear myself up to talk to people and take from them without apparently being able to give anything back. Twenty years later I came back to ethnographic research because I'd become interested in the notion that what people say sounds simple but is in fact complicated. In work concerning people with mental health problems I had observed how very little people who are thought to have such problems are actually listened to. One medical consultant said to me that most professionals are concerned to get services in above everything else. I wanted to document what people with confused speech said as a way of focusing on their status as people, because I thought that this had implications for the way that health and social care workers relate to them. My interest in this issue overcame my reluctance to go and collect data. But when I started the interviews I encountered the same sort of feelings that I'd had many years ago. This time I decided that I needed to work out why I felt guilty and embarrassed, and whether such feelings could be used to explore my data collection in a useful way. I was aware that in counselling, counsellors are encouraged to use their own feelings and performance as a way of exploring their relationship with counsellees. I thought that if I asked what sort of a performance I was putting on and why, it would be useful for my research and for any further personal encounters I had with people with confused speech.

In this chapter I want to explore a paradox in the performance of my research role in this context. It seemed to me that two pulls were operating on me – that of getting good 'juicy' data and the more personal one of being involved in embarrassing situations. These two pulls seem to directly conflict. The very interest of confused speech is its deviance from the norm. To put it crudely, as a novice researcher, I wanted people to be very confused – the more fragmented and disorientated a conversation is, the richer the data (or so it seemed to me to begin with). On the other hand, as a person, I didn't want people to be confused. I wanted to help iron over any difficulties, elide awkwardnesses and reduce any embarrassment to myself and to others to a minimum. This major conflict in my orientation was reproduced in the strategies that the carers and I adopted in the conversations. On the one hand we sought to promote the competence of the person with confused speech so that the conversation proceeded as if it were normal. On the other hand, within the same conversation, we talked across them, thereby emphasizing their incompetence. Thus in these conversations we sought to maintain the identity of the person with confused speech as competent and at the same time emphasized their deviance from competence. Somehow the interview conversations seemed like setting people up. I realized afterwards that I felt very uncomfortable about this, on the grounds cited by Paul Grice: conversation is a co-operative endeavour and as a person one is aware of being unco-operative if one leaves people to stumble along making mistakes (Grice 1975). Yet it was this very deviance for which I was looking.

Given my original research frame, by jointly constructing my data with people with confused speech and their carers, I was faced with being my own worst enemy, trying to paper over the very cracks at which I wanted to look. This realization altered the aim of my research. At the outset I was interested solely in what people with confused speech said – how they broke the rules and so on. As time went by I became equally, if not more, interested in the extent to which those talking to people with confused speech promote the conversation as normal. So the 'papering over the cracks' element became much more central as a direct result of my own recognition of what I found myself doing in the interviews. This analysis draws together the strings of half-formed notions that I had during the interviews. None of the strategies I outline were consciously applied to people with confused speech, although I do think that I learned as I went along how to stage the performance in a more sophisticated way. I also found that theatrical imagery was helpful to me in thinking about the interviews, and I have used it in the rest of the chapter (although not always as a disciplined dramaturgical interpretation *qua* Goffman).

Overture and beginners

My role, as I saw it, was to talk to the person with confused speech, tape recording what I hoped would be a casual conversation. I was introduced to each set of people by the consultant psycho-geriatrician whose clinic they were attending. He explained that I was interested in communication and how they managed with their talking and that I would like to have a brief chat. I then went into a separate room with the person with confused speech and his or her carer. I started off by saying that I wanted to chat to them about their lives. I realize now that I allowed the consultant to get over the awkwardnesses of what I wanted to find out rather than taking responsibility for it myself. I was too embarrassed to say 'I want to talk to you to see how confused you are', although, in fact, most carers did openly discuss how confused their relatives were, in their presence. Instead I used a life history approach as a kind of disguise.

Researcher as actor

I showed everyone my small Walkman tape recorder and asked if they would mind if I used it. When people expressed an interest in it, I asked if they would like to hold it while the interview was going on, which I hoped would be rather like a joint investment in the props of the performance. Several people did hold the recorder (indeed one woman switched it off during the interview while playing with it). In the interviews there seemed to be some dissonance between two roles I was trying to play: as a person holding casual conversation and as a researcher in a formal situation (immediately after the other participants had had a formal interview with the consultant). To cope with this dissonance I found myself underplaying my role as a researcher and emphasizing my role as an ordinary person. I did this in a number of ways. I used some self disclosure in response to the direction of the conversation – where I came from, where I lived, the lives of my friends and relatives, my interests and so on. For example:

Mrs P: (says she has some miniature roses.)
Pam: Do you have to prune them?
Mrs P: No
Pam: I was just wondering because I like roses myself and I've never
         tried any miniature ones and I thought I might get a few hints on
         how to keep them going.

Pam: What sort of cards do you play?
Mr T: Brag
Pam: Brag, for money? (laughs). Pennies, do you win?
Mr T: Sometimes
Pam: Do you? I've been playing cards with some friends now for several
         months and we play for pennies and so far over the whole four
         months I've won twopence. I'm not a very good card player.
         What do you play apart from Brag?

I made no attempt to dramatize my role as researcher (Goffman 1959), bu. I did dramatize my autobiography as material which indicated that I was trying to reciprocate information I was given and to put myself into role as a person as well as a researcher. Thinking about it afterwards I concluded that there were several underlying features to the construction of my personal role. The image I was constructing was as someone who gives back in conversation, who has domestic and social interests that she is willing to throw into the conversational arena, and who takes risks and laughs at herself (i.e. is willing to expose herself). In short, I think that 'the person' that I was performing was someone who has a context and brings a life other than that of the interviewer into the interview. It is interesting to note that I was 'acting' myself whereas most actors 'act' someone else. I suppose the rationale was to offer something as well as to take from the people I was interviewing. In psychology literature (Jourard 1971) self-disclosure is seen as a way of trying to begin to establish a relationship. It's an invitation to reciprocity. At the same time it can be overdone and become a disabling strategy where every experience and fact presented by one conversational participant is capped by the other (Purtilo 1984). In a situation where someone gives you the barest of information, a fulsome response (as in the second extract above) may well have this offputting effect. Perhaps I was putting myself into role as 'a person' too much? Perhaps by doing this I was depressing the conversation rather than stimulating it?

Self-disclosure proved to be an interesting barometer of how I was feeling about myself during the course of the interviews. On each occasion I self-disclosed I came away from the interview feeling like kicking myself. I think my implicit assumption had been that I should allow the onus to be on others to promote the conversation. This is in line with the interviewer's view of the world where the emphasis is on 'them'. There is a feeling that if you contribute too much you'll wipe out what 'they' have to say and this comes back to the conflict between getting good data and being co-operative with other people in conversation.

I also made several confessions of ignorance during these conversations, for example:

Mr H: You were brought up in Evanston weren't you?
Mrs H: Well I got they knew that those people they knew
Pam: They knew
Mrs H: Yes
Pam: What's Evanston like? I've heard of it but I've never been there.

Pam: What was your job Mr T?
Mr T: Capstan operator
Pam: Capstan operator. What does that involve? I don't understand anything about what it does involve

I think such confessions of ignorance served a number of functions, all of which said something more about me as a person:

- to indicate that I didn't know the answer to a question, and therefore that I was not setting the person up (as a teacher may do when she already knows the answers to the questions she asks of a pupil). This may have backed away from the issue of accuracy – if I confessed I didn't know about something, I was unlikely to put the person with confused speech on the spot even if their answer was inaccurate;
- to give myself relatively low status as a person who can be told things – to be given information rather than control it: to emphasize my own naivety and therefore possibly to give higher status to age and experience;
- to indicate that I, too, was uncertain and therefore to normalize the performance of the person suffering from confusion.

Scene stealing

In my conversations the autobiography of the person with confused speech was often jointly constructed with the carer and sometimes solely by the carer (rendering it a biography rather than an autobiography). In this situation the substance of the conversation was taken away from the person with confused speech. In other words, there was some scene stealing going on – sometimes by the carer (sometimes by the carer and myself together). For example, we had been talking about Mrs I's working life:

Pam:	What did they make at Jones's?
Mrs I:	We left there to get jobs
Daughter:	When you left Jones's you went into hosiery to Smith's
Mrs I:	I thought I went to Jones's
Daughter:	No you didn't, you started in Jones's then when you left there you went to Smith's in the hosiery.

This sort of well-intentioned scene stealing raises a number of questions: if you have your performance taken away from you by someone else, power has become an issue. We might say: no performance, no chance of power (except that sometimes refusing to perform can be a very powerful overall disruption of a conversation). Here, however, the performance is taken away from the person with confused speech. Why? My concentration on life history seems to have fostered a desire above everything else for accuracy on the part of all players. Co-operation came to be construed primarily in terms of accuracy.

By the end of the conversation I tended to get a well-constructed biography on behalf of the person with confused speech but nevertheless not one generated by him or her. I think that my attempts at biographical self disclosure were taken, by carers at least, to be a clue as to what 'I wanted' from the conversation. In this situation co-operation to deliver what I wanted came to be the overriding concern and scene stealing became legitimated. I will discuss this more later.

Improvising

While I had some basic plan in my head about using life history as a way of moving the conversation on, in some senses I was improvising throughout the conversation. I found that I was trying to express myself simply in talking to people with confused speech. This was a particularly double-edged sword in my performance. One talks simply when one believes that people may not be able to understand. But often, attempts to achieve simplicity, to improvize for the sake of the conversational flow can lead to less commonplace imagery. For example, when I was talking to one older woman and her carer, I wanted to ask if they had come to the clinic by foot. Since the woman was using a wheelchair I thought the question might be confusing. So instead I found myself saying 'Have you come here on the footpaths today?' Having received no reply to this extraordinary question I still backed off using the notion of coming by foot and asked if they had come by car. I often also tried to put questions in several ways (a feature I also noticed in the tapes I listened to that had been collected by my colleagues). This is a tactic people use when they think that people aren't going to understand. Of course, this tactic can go on in any conversation. However, generally I think it is borne of the anticipation of not getting answers to single questions.

In my role as ordinary person trying to develop an ordinary conversation, I was placed in the situation of needing to do some remedial work to keep the conversation going. Contrary to my expectations of the richness of confused talk (in the sense that, for example, Beckett portrays it in his plays) I found that one of the main features of confused talk was its lack of reciprocity. This remedial work placed me in an invidious situation. I did not want to dominate the conversation (acting the person with confused speech off the stage) because I wanted to hear as much as possible of what they had to say. At the same time my role as conversational participant dictated a certain amount of co-operation in keeping the conversation going. Like the carers I found myself doing everything I could to keep the conversation bowling along. Often this seemed to amount almost to interrogating the person with a barrage of questions as each was fielded back to me with a monosyllabic answer. But even when you know you're doing your best to improvise and keep the conversation going 'as if' normal, it's hard to get away from a feeling that you are dominating in a situation where only monosyllabic answers are coming back (see the first extract on p. 102). You begin to feel your improvisation is a form of scene stealing.

Researcher as director

In looking at my performance I continually find there are two pulls, one towards normalizing the performance of the person with confused speech and one towards an acknowledgement that his or her performance is incompetent. Possibly because of these two pulls I found maintaining my performance rather arduous. I was the one who had started it (as children say), and I did feel that I had to keep the momentum in the conversation going. Whatever the hopes I had harboured of casual reciprocal conversations, it became evident that it was 'my show' and that I was in charge of what was going to be talked about. Certainly the performance of carers indicated that they thought this was so. They were relating to me more in my role as researcher than as a person. As I have suggested, there was a great emphasis on getting the facts straight about the lives of the people with confused speech. The construction of the biography (fuelled by my own self-disclosure) seemed to become the main object of the exercise. When I listened to my tapes afterwards, I found numerous occasions where the carers and I had become carried away with getting the facts straight. In terms of the process of a conversation the co-operation had passed into the hands of the carer and myself, but largely at my direction.

'Dying' on stage

I think my feelings of responsibility in the conversations were heightened by the fact that a number of the people with confused speech to whom I talked had very little conversation and answered mainly in monosyllables. For example, in a conversation about music:

Pam: Do you like country music?
Mrs H: Yeh
Pam: It's very nice isn't it country music?
Mrs H: Yeh
Pam: What are your favourites? (lengthy pause)
Mr H: Crystal chandeliers. It's been on this morning hasn't it?
Mrs H: Yeh
Pam: Has it? Can you sing along with it when it comes on?
Mrs H: Oh yeh
Pam: Do you join in?
Mrs H: Oh yeh (laughs)

In performance there is some obligation to keep both your fellow actors and the audience engaged. When the momentum lies with you as interviewer you may tend to feel that you are an inadequate conversationalist. In most normal conversations people will pick up the intent of even a closed question and will develop an answer which expands beyond the basic question itself. Here my normal reliance on such joint construction of conversation was exposed, and I kept thinking the whole thing must be my fault, that in some way my performance was inadequate. The nadir for me came after I'd been attempting a conversation with a woman who had often only muttered, not even giving monosyllabic answers. Her carer turned to me and said, 'See she's bored now.' So much for my skills as a conversationalist. This seems to be a case of what actors call 'dying' in a performance.

Out of the spotlight

I was only relieved of maintaining the momentum when carers chipped in either by taking over the conversation with the person with confused speech or with stories of their own, largely about their relative, who then became an onlooker. For example:

Mr H: Her dad had got greenhouses of flowers
Pam: Your father had greenhouses?
Mrs H: Yes
Pam: What did he grow in them?
Mr H: You had tomatoes didn't you? Cucumbers
Mrs H: Yeh
Mr H: Chrysanthemums
Mrs H: Yeh
Mr H: And all his bedding plants weren't there?
Mrs H: Yeh

Pam: Are you feeling well at the moment?
Edith: No, I don't know what to do. I don't know

Pam:	What did you think was wrong?
Edith:	(mutters). If I go over there
Son:	It just proves a point here while we've got this tape on that if your system and your body is out of sequence it does affect you
Pam:	Yes
Son:	As I say she's normally still in bed.

Asides

Coping with talking to people with confused speech is hard work. Coping with talking across them is disturbing work. My academic background was one with an emphasis on the personhood of everyone. To talk about people as though they are not there is to reduce them to lesser people. In talking to the person with confused speech I often ended up by responding to the carer who would intervene with correct answers and occasionally tell me in some detail about the progress of their relative's illness. Here the rules of co-operative conversation were stretched beyond co-operation with my main conversational partner, the person with confused speech. I often tried to keep my performance directed towards the person with confused speech, but the imperative to attend to carers was very strong. I do not think that carers intended to make lesser people of those for whom they cared. I think they were rehearsing their own arguments for why things had come to be as they are – possibly justifying the performance they were proffering. In this situation I was, as it were, the recipient of 'asides' – asides to the understanding of the performance. One older man offered to record some conversation between himself and his wife at their home, remarking that 'No one knows what it's like.'

I've already mentioned two roles that I was juggling – that of researcher and that of person. In relation to this notion of carers' asides, I want to mention another now. When carers started to talk to me in what was effectively a separate conversation, I was being offered the role of confidante. Goffman describes a confidante as a person outside the scene of the play (Goffman 1959). A confidante is a person who can receive asides from others. When a carer turned to me and confided some of the problems of interacting with the person with confused speech, this was usually about scenes and situations that had taken place elsewhere. For example, one man described a search for his mother's glasses which had taken place the previous day, offering it as a sort of general comment on situations which happened to them, and how she was always losing everything. There were exceptions to this, as with the man who commented on his mother's performance in the interview itself (see the extract above). But even this was attributed to scenes elsewhere, such as she had had to come to an assessment in the morning and she wasn't generally at her best in the morning.

So while I had assumed that I was going to talk mainly to the person with confused speech and that the 'team' (Goffman 1959) if any, would be him or her and the carer, on numerous occasions the carer broke ranks and became a one-person team, disclosing information destructive to the notion of them as a team. The whole scenario was about management of a spoiled performance (cf. Goffman's book *Stigma: Notes on the Management of Spoiled Identity* 1963). For example:

> *Mr B:*   You can ask her all sorts of things (noises from Mrs B). She won't remember too much at all (noises) some days the mind, I don't know what it is. I wish I did. The mind seems to come alive in a way, if you could call it that and she'll remember things quite well and then perhaps tomorrow or like she's been today as far as memory's concerned its a bad one. I've seen it better. I've seen it better.

What I had stepped into was not only a here and now performance but one of a series of performances, which the carer had learned the person with confused speech could very easily spoil. In the current performance with me as audience I think carers were pre-empting the spoiling of this performance by admitting that spoiled performance was a possibility and that it was not the carer's fault. The invitation was to me as an insider of the current performance and an outsider of previous performances. As an insider I was to team up with them to make allowances now. As an outsider and confidante I was to express sympathy for the plight of those who participated in spoiled performances. The identity of carers was potentially spoiled by association. They needed to distance themselves and to indicate that they recognized that all was not well. I think that this welds together the two contrary features of promoting competence of the confused person and ignoring him or her. Carers and I were doing what we could to maintain a proper performance of a conversation. However, asides in the form of disclaimers (Hewitt and Stokes 1975) were also being offered in case it went wrong. It has also occurred to me that the phenomenon of talking over or across the person with confused speech, while possibly reducing him or her as a person also served the function of diminishing the probability of a spoiled performance. If the person with confused speech was outside the performance then he or she couldn't spoil it (and perhaps thereby save face). Thus the imperative that conversation should work correctly overrules the feelings and status of some of the ostensible participants. The performance subsumes the players.

The final curtain

So what does all this tell me about the process of my research? There are a number of ways in which I think exploring my own performance has helped me. First, it has brought home to me in a very personal way the fact that as qualitative researchers we do construct our data jointly with both research subjects and other people. The notion that it's somehow out there waiting for you to alight on has been exposed as fake. As a novice researcher my fieldwork was living proof of this for me. I played a role in the construction of the research data.

Second, it confirmed to me that one has to be flexible about data. To begin with I was concerned that I wasn't able to talk to people with confused speech in the way that I had hoped. But later I began to realize that the presence of carers and indeed my own performance was something on which I could capitalize. Carers often acted as 'translators' for me, expressing questions to their relatives in a way that enabled them to answer. I wasn't cued into confused speech and could not always understand it – I think this added to my feelings of being an inadequate conversationalist. This gave me valuable insights into how confused speech is construed by normal speakers such as me *and* by normal speakers who have become experienced in interpreting the 'rules' of confused speech. As I said at the beginning of this chapter, my research aims began to change.

Third, I came to see my fieldwork as a learning experience and I was learning not only facts and substance but also roles. I think I learned how to perform better in conversation and to understand that, in having several roles at one's disposal, one may pick up a lot more information than if one is solely a researcher. The juxtaposition of my roles as person, researcher and confidante produced a very rich source of data for me. In examining these identities I had effectively a number of ways of reading the script of the interviews.

Finally, the process of my research led me to begin to think more carefully about the word 'qualitative'. I had always seen qualitative in terms of being a contrast to quantitative. I had not really understood the notion of it as being about people's lives, which they live and which have qualities. Being able to capture the quality of my interactions with people in a research context is something for which I feel I now have a responsibility. My research wasn't merely data to be gathered in but was derived from the stuff of people's lives. I suppose I also now think that there is sometimes quite a big gap between what one aspires to in one's personal role and what one finds oneself doing. At the start of this project I would never have thought that I would be capable of talking over someone whom I considered to be vulnerable and with whom I was supposed to be talking. The imperatives of ordinary social interaction are however very strong. At the end of the fieldwork phase of my research I was left with a feeling of how potent social forces can be.

I also think that even the brief responsibility that I held for keeping the conversation going and the exhaustion that this engendered gave me some insight into how tiring it is to talk frequently to someone where you bear almost the entire burden of the conversation – where any let up in your own performance will threaten a breakdown in the conversation. What for me was a novel experience was for carers a day-in-day-out experience of constant hard work.

Acknowledgement

I should like to thank Martyn Hammersley for reading and commenting on various drafts of this chapter.

9

Interpreting

Moyra Sidell

The question, 'so what are your findings?' is one that sends waves of panic through any researcher's system. If it is asked fairly early in the project then you can hedge with statements like 'I'm still immersed in the data so it's difficult to get the full picture.' But if you are writing up the final report, and it still all seems a bit foggy then you just have to feign coyness and promise to send your enquirer the final report when it is finished. You hope they will then see the full complexity of your argument and realize what a foolish question it was in the first place. However, if you are feeling strong when someone has the audacity to inquire after your findings then what you really need to say is 'it all depends . . .' and launch into a monologue on methodology – how if you take this perspective you could say this, but on the other hand, if you take that perspective then you might say that. All in the end is interpretation.

What I want to do in this chapter is chart an attempt I made to reconcile two interpretations of the health status of older women. These come from different sets of data on the same subject collected under different methodological banners – one positivist and quantitative the other phenomenological and qualitative. The findings conflict: can they both be right?

Background information

When I stumbled on a research career in the mid-1970s, symbolic interactionism was all the rage; the search for meaning was well under way, and it seemed as though we were in the final lurch of a paradigm shift that would topple the positivists for good. In those days we didn't just opt for one particular methodology, we were believers. Our methodology was right –

others were wrong. 'Number cruncher' was the form of abuse we hurled at the positivists. 'Anecdotal' was their retort. And we had our answers ready. Howard Becker's lovely 'scientific mosaic' (1971) was what we were all about, collecting our own bits of blue, grey and maybe even gold to contribute to the grand design. Or we would try them with the less exotic but, we thought, very convincing ideas in 'grounded theory' provided by Glaser and Strauss (1967). We were going out there immersing ourselves in a small area of social life, which we would explore in a totally open-minded fashion, generating substantive theory to feed into the grand design. And we had an answer to hard-nosed statisticians who asked after our 'p' values – our p's related to *people* not probability.

Feminist research entered the fray with work by Ann Oakley (1981), Helen Roberts (1981), Liz Stanley and Sue Wise (1983b) and Sandra Harding (1987) and confirmed our belief in 'soft data'. Moreover we were giving women a voice, we were creating interview situations which allowed for a dialogue, which tried to change the power relationship between researcher and researched. We got involved. We even had delusions of equality.

All this time structuralism and post-structuralism were fermenting, and they were to rock the foundations of our faith. (Those of you interested in these ideas might find Richard Harland's *Superstructuralism*, 1987, Chris Weedon's *Feminist Practice and Poststructuralist Theory*, 1987 and Hal Foster's *Postmodern Culture*, 1985 helpful.) The very meaning of meaning was being questioned and the truthfulness of truth. Was it really a question of interests and power? Who shouts loudest is right because clearly nobody has the right to be right. When everything is socially constructed, one construction is as good as another. Even positivism might have a point.

We adapted. Perhaps we could even learn something from quantitative data. We still preferred our in-depth interviews and biographical data, but the sample survey became speakable. It was in this spirit of tolerance, which some call methodological pluralism, that I embarked on the study which I will describe to you in this chapter.

The point of this book is to be honest and own up to the many irregularities that occur when conducting research but which somehow get ironed out by the final report stage. Retrospective reconstructing goes on in the life history of a research project as much as it does in any other life history. I have to confess that I had not known about 'triangulating' data when I started the project, and it was only at the first draft of the research report that it was brought to my notice. What I had done seemed to fit nicely into that label, with a little adjustment, and so I adopted it as though it had been intended. Instead of simply mixing methods I had been 'triangulating' data. If you want to explore this concept there is an excellent chapter on the topic by Leonie Kellaher, Sheila Peace and Dianne Willcocks in *Researching Gerontology* edited by Sheila Peace (1990). Nigel and Jane Fielding (1986), have also written a monograph on the subject of triangulation called *Linking Data*, and Martyn Hammersley and Paul Atkinson address the concept in *Ethnography: Principles in Practice* (1983). I will give you a brief description drawing largely on these sources.

Triangulating data

Hammersley and Atkinson claim that the term derives from navigation and surveying – the geographical kind. They explain:

> For someone wanting to locate their position on a map, a single landmark can only provide the information that they are situated somewhere along a line in a particular direction from that landmark. With two landmarks, however, their exact position can be pinpointed by taking bearings on both landmarks.
>
> (Hammersley and Atkinson 1983: 198)

Triangulating data is a multi-dimensional approach to collecting and analysing data. Four main types of triangulation are identified – investigator triangulation where more than one person examines the same situation; theory triangulation, which uses different theoretical perspectives; triangulating the data in terms of time, space and person; and methodological triangulation (Fielding and Fielding 1986 and Kellaher et al. 1990).

It was the last one, methodological triangulation, that I think I was doing. I see this as very different from using different methods within the same methodological framework. For instance, the first project I worked on, investigating consumer views of Day Centres for older people (Fennell et al. 1981), used in-depth biographical interviews with individual older users of the Day Centres, conducted in their own homes, and also participant observation in the Day Centres. Both of these methods come within the qualitative framework. In my present study I was analysing data collected in both the quantitative and qualitative methodological frameworks. This was similar although less ambitious than the examples of triangulation described by the Fieldings in their study of police recruit training (1986) and by Leonie Kellaher and her colleagues in their study of consumers in 100 local authority old people's homes. Both these studies carried out sample surveys in the quantitative tradition and then focused on a sub-sample for in-depth enquiry. Both used participant observation, the Fieldings in police education and instruction settings and Leonie Kellaher and colleagues in a sub-sample of homes. They both drew on the perspectives of different actors in the situations, staff and residents in the homes, recruits and instructors in the police setting. Although much broader in scope than my own study, the crucial element was the same – the use of both quantitative and qualitative data to understand the same subject matter. This is where triangulating data becomes problematic because mixing methods is also about mixing interpretations.

Different research methods are not simply different *ways of doing*, they also represent different *ways of seeing* and *ways of thinking*. Quantitative methods are based broadly on the philosophy of positivism. This views the world, and, in the case of the social sciences, the social world, as definable in terms of certain laws which are open to observation. What you see is what you get. And if you can count what you see then you know what you've got.

Qualitative methods arise from a different philosophical tradition, one which looks for meaning behind social action. This involves more than observing the social world, it requires interaction with the social world. As researcher you must be part of the process, you need to understand the symbolic nature of social action in the search for meaning.

If research methods are based on radically different versions of the world then can one simply mix and match with equanimity? And can a habituated qualitative researcher learn (mathematics and statistics notwithstanding) to be a quantitive researcher and vice versa? I think it is possible, but inevitably, s/he will bring some qualitative or quantitative baggage along.

Interpretation is not only involved at the final stages of a research study it is also involved at the data collection and data analysis stages. In relation to data collection, Social Community Planning and Research (SCPR) used to maintain that interviewers were either good at administering a pre-coded interview in the quantitative tradition or at carrying out an unstructured or semi-structured in-depth interview, but it was rare that someone was able to do both. I can vouch for that. In hard times I have taken on survey interviewing and made a complete mess of it, allowing the respondent to stray off the point, not being able to fit their response into an appropriate box and generally losing control of the interview.

In this study I was triangulating data only at the analysis stage, performing secondary analysis on large nationally collected sample survey data as well as using published national statistics. The idea was to compare these data sets with the information I got from biographical interviews with older women. I will explain to you something about these different data sets and some of the interpretive problems involved in the secondary analysis before going on to the problems of interpreting the different 'findings' which they exposed.

What did I do?

I was investigating the health status of older women; I used three levels of investigation, spanning quantitative and qualitative methods.

The three levels of data ranged from very 'hard' to very 'soft'. They were:

1 national statistics on mortality and morbidity;
2 data from two large scale sample surveys;
3 biographical interviews with 30 older women which I carried out myself.

What exactly did they amount to?

National Statistics on Mortality and Morbidity

Mortality statistics[1]

From these I could work out the causes of death of women over the age of 65 in a given year. I could tell, for example, the proportions who died of cancer of the lung compared to those who died of heart disease. I could also break down the very large age category of over-65 into three sub-categories: people aged 65–74; those 75–84; over 85. This allowed me to compare cause of death for people aged 65–74 compared with those aged over 85. Information is available on social class, but the social classification of women, especially older women, is so fraught with difficulty that it is hard to feel confident about the data. Fox and Goldblatt's (1982) 'Longitudinal study of mortality differentials' addresses these issues if you are interested. The statistics do give information on marital status, and I was able to compare the causes of death of single women compared to married women. I could, of course, compare men with women on all those age and marital status groupings in terms of the causes of death.

Morbidity statistics
Here I used three different sources –

The Hospital In-patient Enquiry[2]
The information it provides is the diagnosis, age and sex of all those who died or were discharged from hospital in a given year. So I could tell how many women over the age of 65 were in hospital, and with what diagnosis, in the year under study. Again this can be broken down into sub-groups according to age. Unfortunately they do not give any information on marital status, social class or ethnicity and so the comparisons are limited to age groups and sex.

The Mental Health Enquiry[3]
It provides much the same information regarding mental illness as the Hospital In-Patient Enquiry. I was able to compare the number of men who were hospitalized for, say, depression in a given year compared to the number of women, and again to break this down by age categories.

Morbidity statistics from General Practice[4]
This provides information on consultations and episodes of illness on all patients in a given year. The information includes age, sex and diagnosis. From this I could find out which complaints older women were taking to their doctors and compare them to the complaints of older men. I could also compare men and women in terms of age categories.

   These sources provide statistical evidence, 'hard data', on causes of death and prevalence of different diseases by age and sex and, in some cases, other socio-economic categories (although marital status was the only other variable which I found useful). The data is not available for secondary analysis, and I was therefore limited to the categories they analyse.

National Sample Survey Data

The General Household Survey[5]
This is a wide ranging survey which supplies information on about 1000 variables to a number of government departments including employment, education, housing and health. Different years concentrate on special issues, for instance in 1985 the survey included questions about informal care. The raw data is available for secondary analysis through the Economic and Social Research Council (ESRC) Data Archive at Essex University. This enables individual researchers to follow up

their own concerns (for anyone interested in secondary analysis Angela Dale, Sara Arber and Michael Procter 1988, have written a useful guide). I was able to cross-tabulate certain socio-economic variables (such as age, sex, social class, marital status, level of education, housing tenure, whether people had borne children, or whether they had worked outside the home) with information which was of interest to my study such as, prevalence of chronic illness and disability, self assessments of health, visits to the doctor and days in bed due to sickness.

The Health and Lifestyles Survey[6]

The survey included questions about the prevalence of disease, disability and symptoms – both physical and mental – that the respondent had experienced in the month prior to the interview. In the interviews people were asked to rate their own health and they were asked questions to elicit their health beliefs and attitudes. Certain tests such as blood pressure measurements, tests of lung capacity and memory tests were conducted on the respondents and they were asked questions about their health behaviour. This data was also available for secondary analysis so I was able to draw out information which related to the older people in the sample.

Although these two sample surveys fall within the area of quantitative methods, they are different from the mortality and morbidity statistics discussed above. The difference lies in the fact that they represent the self-report of the sample. People are asked questions about themselves to which they supply the answer. However, they usually have to fit their replies into a limited range of pre-coded options. The General Household Survey operates with only pre-coded questions, but the Health and Lifestyles Survey left many of their questions 'open' and coded them retrospectively. By doing this they were not prejudging the range of replies that people might come up with. This could perhaps be described as hard data with a soft centre, or 'medium textured' data.

Biographical interviews

My third type of data was firmly in the qualitative 'soft' arena and consisted of biographical interviews with 30 older women. Thirty was the number I felt I could manage in terms of time and resources. It was far too small a sample to pretend to be representative, but I did have a spread of age-groups. The social class distribution was roughly in line with the general population of older women as was the marital status breakdown. Most of the women were living in their own homes, but two were residents in an old people's home, two in very sheltered housing schemes and five in warden-controlled flats or bungalows. They were from a mixture of urban and rural settings, but only two of the women I interviewed were from ethnic minorities, and they were both of Afro-Caribbean origin. The interviews were tape-recorded and then transcribed. They were unstructured, but focused interviews, which invited respondents to discuss their health, and their beliefs and attitudes to health within the context of their present and past experience. Most interviews lasted for about two hours. The shortest was half an hour, cut short by the arrival of a visitor. The longest lasted about seven hours in all and was conducted over several visits.

Interpreting and analysing

It became apparent that my approach to secondary analysis was coloured by my predilection for qualitative methodology and the way I interpret the social world. Let me give you one example. In order to carry out secondary analysis on the survey data I dutifully learnt the SPSSX formulae (the statistical package for the social sciences) and performed quite sophisticated cross-tabulations. But when helpful statisticians who taught me these techniques urged me to perform 'multiple regression analysis' on the data to isolate the variable which correlates most with the health status of older women I could sense that my eyes glazed over and my nod was polite rather than enthusiastic. Maybe it was the limitations of my grasp of statistics, but I prefer to think it was my interactive view of the world that spurred me to find the range and breadth of variables which were associated with the health status of older women rather than to seek for one variable that might account for their health status.

I believe that quantitative researchers find it equally hard to surrender their positivistic tendencies when dealing with qualitative data. A recent text written for the purpose, *Qualitative Data Analysis* (Miles and Huberman 1984), suggests a formidable array of techniques to reduce qualitatitve data to graphs, pie-charts and bar diagrams and thus make it quantitatively respectable. Perhaps it is early days yet in terms of methodological triangulation, and a new breed of researchers will, and probably already have, emerged who are untainted by previous beliefs. But my own experience indicates that letting go of once strongly held convictions is not easy.

Why do it? What did I hope to gain by 'triangulating data' in this way? Again I quote Leonie Kellaher et al. who maintained that: 'triangulation essentially implies a meeting and meshing of different boundaries for a given topic which enables questions to be posed in new ways, leading to fresh insights and understanding' (Kellaher et al. 1990: 120).

What I hoped to do was to use the different levels of data to home in on the subject of the health status of older women, gradually putting more flesh on the skeletal structure of the statistical data. I did hope for 'fresh insights and understanding', but it was not as straightforward as that, and I would wholeheartedly agree with Martyn Hammersley and Paul Atkinson's view that:

> One should not, therefore, adopt a naively 'optimistic' view that aggregation of data from different sources will unproblematically add up to produce a more complete picture . . . differences between sets of data may be just as important and illuminating.
>
> (1983: 199)

Interpreting the evidence

What I found was a mass of paradox and downright contradictory evidence. The hard data presents a picture of older women living a long time, diseased both mentally and physically, forever taking to their beds and bothering their doctors with trivial matters. The 'medium textured' data shows older women admitting to a good deal of symptomatology but assessing their health optimistically. The soft data presents a picture of older women as resilient and full of stamina, not giving in to aches and pains, rarely taking to their beds and extremely reluctant to visit their doctors. All this is very much reflected in two competing myths which vie for credibility in the gerontological world. One myth, which is broadly a medicalized version, sees older people and particularly older women as having generally poor health status. The other myth has older people remaining fit and healthy until they suffer from the illness from which they die. This is the version preferred by social gerontologists who are keen to counter ageist attitudes by presenting a more positive view of old age. Evidence to support both myths can be summoned which convinces neither camp, for, like all myths, they are not untruths or just fantasy, each is the truth from a particular perspective. So attempts to invalidate or discredit one myth and replace it with another have been unfruitful and unproductive.

So what can be made of this paradox, how is one to interpret the contradictions? I offer you two interpretations, one straightforward and plausible the other a bit more fanciful.

The straightforward interpretation

If we inhabit a socially constructed world then we cannot take the meaning of health for granted. Health is a very ephemeral concept, one which we think we can grasp yet find hard to define. Nor can we assume that what I see as good health is what you see as good health. It has become a much contested concept with biomedical definitions being challenged by a more social model of health which takes into account the wider social and physical environment. The very hard data operates within a biomedical framework which sees good health as the absence of disease; on this basis older women are full of disease which limits their activity. But how do older women interpret the meaning of health? What is it that they are saying when they assert that their health is good?

The Health and Lifesyles Survey asked respondents what it felt like when they were healthy. Table 9 shows their responses, broken down by age and sex.

Table 9 What it is to be healthy

	Women %		Men %	
	65–74 yrs n=592	Over 75 yrs n=344	65–74 yrs n=448	Over 75 yrs n=231
Can't explain	9	14	8	8
Have no disease	10	13	16	16
Have physical energy	14.5	9	12	9
Able to do things	29	33	26	28
Feel good	57	44	55	51

Note: Individuals frequently gave more than one answer so columns do not total 100.
Source: Health and Lifestyle Survey (Cox and Blaxter et al. 1987) and own analysis of unpublished data.

Well over half the men and women under 75 years expressed their health in terms of feelings. But this was less so for the very elderly women who were more inclined to think in terms of doing things.

Feelings were definitely on the health agenda of the 30 older women I interviewed about their health (Sidell 1991). What was clear from the interviews was that individuals can hold a range of views on health which encompass physical and emotional elements. Health certainly was not a one-dimensional concept and the range of attitudes and beliefs about health formed a continuum as follows:

Physical/functional–emotional–psychological/spiritual

For instance, a 67-year-old woman who lived on a council estate in Brixton, had an exercise bike in the corner of her room because she felt exercise was good for her health. But she had an appealing philosophy that good health was to do with making people happy: 'Well, I think good health is when you can laugh and make people laugh. People say riches is money, but riches is when you can laugh and make someone happy.' However, she maintained that people used to be healthier because they did not have chemicals in their food. She then described her own health in terms of strength which was a gift from the gods – in her case a non-conformist Christian god in whom she had a deep faith: 'I think he puts a lively spirit into you, make you lively, and gives you strength. He really has given me an excess of strength.'

Another interviewee, who was 94-years-old and lived in a private residential home had a very rich perspective on health. For her health was synonymous with being human, and her understanding of human was threefold as she explained:

> You find out what a human being is, what makes a human being tick, so there are three things; there is the will, there is the feeling and there is the thinking and if you bring harmony into willing, feeling and thinking, you have a nice human being.

Central to her understanding of life, health included, was a concept of destiny which was tied to a strong belief in reincarnation. It was a process of development which began before, and would go on after this life. Her concept of destiny was not fatalistic, she believed in a 'law of consequences' – what you did yesterday certainly has consequences for today. The course of development was not fixed: 'I believe that we come with a certain amount of basic ground. There's good ground, and not so good ground, the possibilities to develop.' She has spent much of her extreme old age trying to understand and make sense of her life and how she had developed into what she now describes herself – an 'extremely tough' person. This was from inauspicious beginnings: 'I was the least strong-looking and healthy-looking child of my mother, and I am the last surviving of the lot.'

This was no accident, she believed. She has been, not only a most sickly child, but the middle one of three and in her view the least valued. But she said, 'That didn't make me angry and it didn't make me aggressive and revengeful or timid – no, it gave me strength.'

Strength was very much a feature of most of the women's views of health; weakness was associated with ill health. These were not just physical dimensions, they were more to do with 'grit': determination, stamina and willpower. Health was defined by the women I interviewed in much wider terms than the absence of disease or the ability to function – it was very much a multi-faceted concept. If health has many meanings then it is hardly surprising that measuring it is likely to be fraught with difficulty and that the evidence will conflict. This interpretation that the thing being measured is open to interpretation is an explanation which relates particularly to concepts like health. The next interpretation I want to offer has, I think, a wider appeal.

The speculative interpretation

The tension between statistical aggregate data which relates to populations and the experience of people who make up that population is fascinating. The average person derived from aggregate data describes everyone, but no actual real person. What then is the relationship between statistics about people and the people involved? If they contradict each other what are we to make of that? Can they be reconciled?

On the basis that a little knowledge is a liberating thing, I offer you this interpretation which I make from my very limited knowledge of quantum physics. It relates to that bit of quantum physics that has percolated into popular ideas, the relationship between the wave and the particle. It seems that a wave of light is not a simple undulating line, it is made up of numerous particles which are constantly darting about and changing position relative to each other although remaining in, and indeed determining, the path of the wave. The wave represents their collective direction, but each particle follows a much more haphazard path.

The image of a wave of light going up and down because of the movement of particles put me in mind of visual representations of statistical evidence, such as graphs and scatter diagrams where you plot a path through the individual dots. The line is determined by the path of the dots, but they do not form a simple line and are more like a band with some above the line and some below, so the line does not correspond directly to individual dots especially if they move about.

If we take the statistical evidence on the health status of older women in general as the wave, and the health status of individual older women as the particles, then we can have two versions which, whilst seeming to contradict, are in fact part of the same picture. The wave or curve shows a large number of older women to be in a poor state of health but within that curve each individual older women's health fluctuates and changes, darting about like the particles of light described in quantum physics. It is not fixed like a statistic but is constantly moving. The following diagrams, will, I hope, illuminate schematically what I am trying to say. What I would really like to do is to show moving diagrams, but that is not possible. You will have to use your powers of

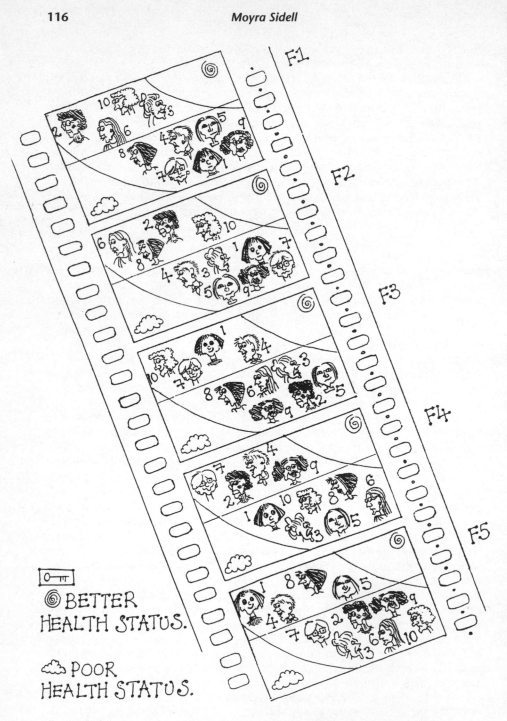

Figure 9 Health status of older women. (Drawings by Louise Partridge.)

imagination to see that each of the diagrams marked F1, F2, F3, F4 and F5 is like one frame from a moving picture. The time scale is irrelevant, it could be five days, five weeks, five months etc. – it is a state of fluidity that I am trying to capture.

In reality we would be dealing with thousands of older women, but for the sake of convenience let's pretend that the population of older women is only ten. Each numbered head in the diagrams represents the health status of one older woman. I have drawn actual heads in the diagrams to make the whole thing more human, but that may be misleading because it is really the health status which is the particle not each older woman.

You will notice that while there are always more at the 'poor health' end of the curve they are not always the same numbers. There are always six out of the ten women in the area of poor health at any one time therefore on balance for that population of older women, their health is poor. But only women 3, 5 and 9 spend most of their time in the area of poor health and even they are not entirely there. The rest are constantly moving and so their experience is not described by the whole.

This explanation is similar but subtly different from that between cross-sectional and longitudinal analysis. If you made the statistical analysis at different time periods, you would still get the same overall picture. The proportions of older women in poor health would remain similar. But they would be different older women going in and out of poor health.

My interpretation is, I would emphasize, only speculative – it is an offering and certainly does not have QED status. I would doubt if it could be proved or disproved mathematically because of the difficulty of dealing with unpredictably moving targets. However, statisticians do deal with complicated problems inherent in measures of central tendency (it would be fascinating if anyone wanted to take it further). All that I claim to be doing is making an analogy with the 'wave and particle' theory as a way of understanding why, when viewed collectively, older women seem to suffer from poor health, yet individually most of them claim not to.

If I put my two interpretations together then we have quite a complex picture. The probability is that most women will suffer a good deal of chronic illness and disability in old age but, because this will fluctuate for each individual older woman, it will not determine her own overall experience of her health status. This is much more fluid and further complicated because how she perceives her health status is bound up with how she interprets the concept of health. Both myths are thus accommodated by this interpretation.

No doubt you could offer different interpretations of my dilemma. Research frequently throws up more questions than it answers and in so doing manages to perpetuate the process. Every good research report ends with a section on the need for further research in the hope of persuading the funders that the answer is just over the next hill – and any good fell walker knows what is always over the next hill.

It is not without a tinge of nostalgia that I look back on the days of methodological puritanism. Interpreting was a lot simpler then. You were not required to perform intellectual contortions, and we qualitative types didn't have to do our sums. On the other hand, at least methodological pluralism makes a nonsense of the idea of finding anything that will fit on one side of an A4 sheet of paper, and clearly there are some methods which are more appropriate for certain tasks. But I think it would be sad if the gains to be had from methodological tolerance were made at the expense of methodological commitment. I would therefore echo the point made by Fiona Williams that it is important to be an 'ist' and committed, but not to let the 'ism' rule.

Notes

1. Here I used the annual statistics on mortality published by the Office of Population Censuses and Surveys (OPCS) which give information on cause of death, age, sex and marital status.
2. This source is also published annually by OPCS. It provides information on all discharges and deaths from NHS hospitals in England and Wales.
3. This is again published by OPCS and is similar to the Hospital in-patient enquiry but is confined to Mental Illness Hospitals.
4. This is a survey of 51 General Practices who volunteered to take part in the study. So far there have been three such surveys – one in 1971, another in 1976 and another in 1982.
5. This is a survey carried out annually by the OPCS. It is a nationally representative sample of about 10,000 private households with about 25,000 individuals in all. It includes about 9000 people over the age of 65.
6. This was a one-off national sample survey of adults in England, Wales and Scotland conducted by the Office of the Regius Professor of Physics and the Department of Psychiatry, University of Cambridge School of Clinical Medicine. In all 9003 iindividuals were interviewed, including about 2000 people over the age of 65.

10

Telling

Sally French

In this chapter I will draw on my experiences, and those of other researchers and writers, to explore the ways in which research data is shaped in the processes of writing, publication and dissemination. As researchers we must decide what we are prepared to reveal about ourselves, the methods we use, and the people we investigate. We may enter what can be a long and arduous process of negotiation with those who judge and assess our work. If our research is eventually accepted for publication, we must accept that further shaping may occur in the editing processes, and that control of the information may be lost. Given the fact that only a limited number of words are allowed when writing an article, a research report or a book, we must also make choices, and will tend to select those aspects of our work which appear most interesting and newsworthy. The content of this chapter, on how our research is told, is inevitably shaped by my own experiences as an academic researcher and writer working within the fields of disability and physiotherapy. Contract research and research in other disciplines gives rise to different problems which are outside my experience.

Deciding what to tell

In this section I will highlight the many dilemmas I, and other researchers, face when deciding what to tell and what to conceal of our research.

The legitimacy of information

One problem I have encountered when undertaking research, is whether to disclose information which is given by research participants outside the research context. This dilemma originates from my education in psychology, where 'objectivity' is viewed as fundamental to 'good' research. When interviewing disabled health and caring professionals about their experiences at work (French 1986a), for example, I have frequently found that they tell me more over a meal or while walking to the railway station after the interview than during the interview itself. They also ask me questions which open up interesting lines of enquiry far removed from those on my carefully planned interview schedule. One or two people have even contacted me later to ask for advice with employment difficulties.

Being a disabled person and a health professional myself, the social distance between us is minimal, which encourages this open communication. In this situation I have to decide whether it is legitimate to include the informally gathered information in my research report, and whether to attempt to be objective about a culture of which I am so clearly a part. The 'cookbooks' of research methodology rarely address these issues, let alone give any advice, though some texts on feminist and qualitative research are more helpful, for example Graham (1984) and Ely et al. (1991).

Ensuring anonymity and confidentiality

In 1989 I interviewed a sample of visually impaired physiotherapists to learn about their situation at work (French 1989a). They comprised a very close-knit group, and being a visually impaired physiotherapist myself, I had much in common with them; I knew many of them personally and had been through many similar experiences. Not only was the problem of being 'objective' intensified in this situation, but new dilemmas arose which no textbook ever addresses. Many of the physiotherapists knew each other intimately, not only through work and college connections, but from their early childhood days in special residential schools. They were constantly asking me for information about each other, and on more than one occasion I was given information which conflicted with the content of the 'real' interview. The research is for my doctorate, where it is perhaps necessary to follow certain rules and conventions and to justify what I do. But how do I cope with the rule of confidentiality in this situation without alienating the research participants? Which version of the truth should I tell? What indeed is the truth, and is there ever just one version of it? These issues are discussed in some depth by Dean and Foote Whyte (1978).

Protecting the anonymity of research participants can also become problematic at the stage of publication and dissemination. Some of the health and caring professionals I interviewed for an MSc dissertation (French 1986a), for example, were very unusual – a doctor with spina bifida, a profoundly deaf occupational therapist, a blind social worker. Names of people, places and people's gender, can, of course, be changed, although this may be insufficient to protect their anonymity (Plummer 1983). The researcher is faced with a considerable dilemma, because by preserving the anonymity of the research participants some distortion of the truth may be necessary, leading the readership to be deceived.

Unethical methods

If research methods which may be considered unethical are used, the re-searcher may choose to conceal them or not to publish the work at all. As part of my research on the situation of disabled health and caring professionals (French 1986a), I wrote letters and made telephone calls to professional organizations pretending to be a careers officer enquiring on behalf of disabled clients. I did reveal the method when I published the research, but fears of professional harm caused me more than a passing qualm, and I have frequently been asked to justify my use of these methods. This I have done by pointing out the improbability of gaining truthful information, in an open and honest way, from powerful people in society whose attitudes and behaviour reduce the opportunities of those who are disadvantaged and marginalized.

Protecting oneself and the research participants

As researchers we may deliberately omit some of our findings, for example, we may conceal aspects of our research which went wrong, or attempt to protect the research participants by hiding information which could be used against them. Some research I undertook (which has yet to be fully analysed), wherein I investigated the work situation of visually impaired physiotherapists (French 1989a), has left me wondering whether some of the things the participants revealed, for example, the difficulties they experience with certain aspects of their role, could harm them professionally if they were exposed or, conversely, whether such exposure could serve to enlighten those in power. Researchers may also feel reluctant to talk critically of the people who have participated in their research so willingly. If information which is likely to offend is omitted, then rather bland results may be produced, though some feminists believe that researchers have a duty to advocate for their female research participants rather than revealing damaging information about them (Finch 1984).

External constraints on telling

Smith (1978) has spoken of gatekeepers in the academic community, those individuals and bodies – editors, experts, advisers, reviewers, journal committees – who decide which articles to accept for publication, which to reject and how those which are accepted should be altered. The knowledge that is produced is thus selected and 'shaped' by those in power. This process may serve to maintain the *status quo* and protect professional interests, creating enormous problems for those bent on innovation and challenging conventional ideas. Spender (1981) notes that most gatekeepers are men which creates a further barrier for women researchers, especially those working within a feminist framework.

The process of selecting articles for publication can be far from honest or fair. Those of us serving as editors and assessors may, sometimes unwittingly, reject work which challenges our own ideas and writings, as well as those of respected members of the academic or professional community. Mahoney (1977) found that papers were more likely to be accepted for publication if the results accorded with the assessors' biases, and Broad and Wade (1982) believe that peer review can act like an 'old boy system'. Making sure that the reference list contains the work of established figures can sometimes assist with publication, as Shipman (1988) puts it, 'The reference is a neat way of combining flattery with erudition.' In addition, publishers are motivated by financial considerations and are likely to be more interested in how well books sell than in what they contain.

Application forms for academic appointments often require the applicant to list 'referenced' articles only (those which have been subjected to peer review) with little interest being taken in other publications which may have reached many more people. Authors and researchers may also be under pressure to use referenced material when writing articles and books. In a recent and favourable review of a book I edited (French 1992a), I was criticized for using information from unreferenced material (Richardson 1992). Even the references at the end of an article can cause alarm and disquiet; on one occasion I was asked by a journal editor if one of my references, entitled 'Professionalised Service and Disabling Help' (McKnight 1981) was a joke!

In this section I will use my own experience and that of other writers and researchers to explore the external pressures which influence what we are able to tell. Because I will focus on difficulties and problems, this may be perceived as rather negative, or as a continual string of misfortunes. It should be emphasized, however, that the advice of editors and reviewers is often well meant and can be extremely valuable. Many of my articles have been greatly improved by their comments, suggestions, and criticisms, and I try, when asked to review papers myself, to help authors rather than hinder them, although I am acutely aware of at least some of my biases. Most of the papers I have submitted for publication have been accepted without great difficulty, and the confidence that reviewers and editors have shown in my work has enhanced my self-confidence and self-esteem, and induced me to continue writing. Thus, the incidents I relate are rather unusual, though very memorable, events.

The peer review system

My first brush with the peer review system occurred with the very first article I attempted to publish in 1985. It was a critique of a system of assessment used by physiotherapists and other health professionals, called 'The problem orientated medical record' (POMR) which was gaining popularity at that time. I sent the article, which was well researched, to *Physiotherapy*, the journal of the Chartered Society of Physiotherapy. The reply which I received was both curt and disapproving. I had revealed the fact that, despite my serious misgivings with the POMR system (which I had taught to physiotherapy students for some time), I did not have lengthy experience of using it practically. This information was used as a way of discrediting my arguments and rejecting the article.

Although I understood the likely reasons for this speedy and outright rejection of an article I had prepared with great care, as it was my first, my confidence was shaken, and I could not bring myself to submit it elsewhere, or even to read it again. As a consequence it lay untouched for six years at the bottom of a drawer. In the meantime I was having considerable success publishing other articles, several in *Physiotherapy*, and had also become a peer reviewer for the journal myself. Then one Sunday afternoon, having gained confidence as a writer and having nothing better to do, I re-read the article and was pleasantly surprised that it did not seem too bad. With a little up-dating, re-shaping and cutting I submitted it to the 'lightweight', less conservative newspaper *Therapy Weekly* and had an immediate very positive response from the editor saying how stimulating he found it and how he would publish it without delay, which he duly did (French 1991a). The article has also been published in an Open University Reader (Swain et al. 1993).

Perhaps the lapse of time had something to do with these differing responses, but I do not believe this to be a major factor. In my view the difference lies within the nature of the publications I approached. *Therapy Weekly* is more likely to publish controversial articles and does not have a peer review system; it is quite likely that one of the people whose work I criticized in the article I submitted to *Physiotherapy* was one of my assessors! Editors of popular newspapers, unlike those of professional journals, tend to like sensational items and unusual or outrageous opinions, as Skyte (1990) states, 'any physiotherapist who believes and is prepared to say that exercise is bad for you and being fat is healthy is virtually guaranteed to get into the national press.'

Authors are not usually anonymous although the assessors and reviewers of their work often are. The appointment of assessors and reviewers is not typically open or advertised but rather is based on a system of contacts and friendships. This means that the influence of editors can penetrate deeply into the reviewing system, as these contacts and friends are likely to share ideas and perspectives similar to those of the editors themselves. This gives rise to a bias towards accepting articles written by those who are known and respected, and a corresponding tendency to reject articles from little known researchers and writers. In the journal *Physiotherapy* it is openly acknowledged that the qualifications of potential authors play a role when considering their articles for publication (*Physiotherapy* November 1991). Some editorial groups, for example those of *Critical Social Policy, Spare Rib* and *Feminist Review*, however, have made strenuous efforts to promote equal opportunities, for example, by ensuring that membership is extended to substantial numbers of women and black people. Expanding practice of this kind could be an important way forward in resolving many of the problems of assessment and peer review.

The 'rules' of research

Telling the truth when submitting an article can be a dangerous move. In 1991 Susan Neville, a physiotherapy lecturer, and I, submitted an article to *Physiotherapy* regarding students' and clinical supervisors' views about clinical education in physiotherapy (Neville and French 1991). The data had been collected for purposes other than research, and we did not, at the time of collecting it, intend to write a paper. The students' views on clinical education were gathered by asking them to write a short essay on what, in their view, constituted a 'good' and a 'poor' clinical experience, in the hope that their ideas could be used to improve clinical education. The clinical tutors' views were gathered as a learning activity during a workshop on clinical education. Susan Neville was carrying out some research in clinical education at the time, and I had recently written a chapter on the subject for a book; we both noticed how closely the students' and the clinical tutors' views tallied with the findings of what little research existed on the subject.

We felt it only proper to be honest and to explain how the paper had come to be written. Before describing the methodology, we explained the origins of the paper confessing that, 'for this reason the research methodology was less rigorous than it would ideally be'. In the next edition of *Physiotherapy* there was a letter written by a physiotherapist involved in research which read:

> Neville and French state that their method is 'less rigorous than it would ideally be' but I would suggest to you that research is by definition a rigorous activity. If it is not rigorous it is not research and should not be published as a research paper. Scientific journals use criteria such as lack of rigour to reject submitted papers. Until *Physiotherapy* does so as well it can have no hope of inclusion in *Index Medicus*.
>
> (Alexander 1991: 387)

It would appear that following the 'scientific rules' of research, and gaining status within that culture, is, for some people at least, more important than the knowledge which is generated. It should be emphasized, however, that the article went through the peer review system without difficulty, reflecting considerable changes of attitude towards research in the physiotherapy profession.

Which methodology?

The insistence by some journal editors and assessors that articles and research papers should be of a certain type, also serves to shape the knowledge produced in that particular field. If, for example, a journal committee rejects research papers based on 'naturalistic' methods, a valuable source of knowledge will be lost. This can be a serious problem for professions whose practice draws on many branches of knowledge, such as the paramedical professions, and is particularly likely to affect small professions which are represented by only one or two journals. Until very recently the guidelines for writing articles in *Physiotherapy* were entirely in terms of experimental research, with a strong expectation that statistics would be used to analyse the data. The tone has now begun to change, and there have recently been several articles in the journal discussing the meaning of research and advocating a broad range of methods (Parry 1991; Stone 1991).

It can, however, be difficult in disciplines such as psychology, physiotherapy and medicine to get results published which are not statistically significant (Carver 1978; Broad and Wade 1982; French 1988). The statistically significant result is therefore likely to stand unopposed and out of context. Similarly, studies reporting success, for example, the success of behaviour modification programmes, are more likely to be published than those demonstrating failure.

No doubt one of the appeals of statistical analyses, as a means of 'telling', is their numerical presentation and the fact that they are perceived as being part of the scientific enterprise which is viewed with such trust and valued so highly by many sectors of our society at the present time. The view that statistics and statistical significance are so important is encouraged by many research methodology texts. Harris (1986), for example, states that, 'Choosing the correct statistical test is the key to the whole process of finding out exactly what your data have to tell you.' This sort of advice can culminate in funding bodies and researchers failing to consider important issues which are not amenable to statistical analysis. In addition, many statistical tests are very complicated and difficult even for statisticians to comprehend, and their use, along with jargon, can be a form of censorship or a means of creating professional and academic barriers and mystique.

Censorship

Research can undergo censorship in more direct ways. In 1987 I sent an article to *Physiotherapy* concerning the attitudes of physiotherapists to the recruitment of disabled people into that profession (French 1987). It was based on an MSc dissertation I had written on the situation of disabled health and caring professionals (French 1986a). Contained within the article was the following paragraph taken from the physiotherapy careers literature of 1984:

> Any form of physical disability or weakness is likely to contra-indicate physiotherapy as a suitable career, in particular defects in hearing, epilepsy, chest ailments, skin conditions, heart defects, nervous breakdowns, injuries to backs, knees and hands may also prejudice acceptance for training.
>
> (French 1984: 387)

The article was accepted and published, but only on the condition that I omitted this paragraph, which I reluctantly agreed to do, even though it had been the main stimulus for undertaking the study.

Who does the telling?

The phenomenon whereby the views of certain sections of society are dominant, while others are distorted or ignored, has been challenged in feminist research. Spender (1985: 221) points out that women have far less time to write, in our society, than men. She states, 'That men are serviced while women do the servicing is a critical consideration in the working conditions for writing.' Disseminating research findings is rarely written into research contracts and researchers usually find that the telling must be done in their own time. The white, male-dominated, able-bodied structures and hierarchies within publishing, research and academia, mean that the knowledge base of many disciplines has been constructed largely by white men, with the voice of women, black people and disabled people being barely audible.

The exclusion of those who are being researched from the research process is particularly harmful. A current example of this is the struggle disabled people are engaged in to shift the meaning of disability from that of individual impairment (an assumption under-pinning much research on disability) to that of social barriers and social oppression (Oliver 1987; French 1992b). When talking of women, Spender (1985: 192) points out that oppressed groups become a potential source of danger when they write because 'they are in a position to articulate a subversive doctrine'. Many writers and researchers are, however, striving to correct this tendency by actively involving disabled people in their research and writings (Atkinson and Williams 1990; Taylor and Bishop 1991; Swain et al. 1993). See also the chapters by Dorothy Atkinson, Joanna Bornat, and Ann Brechin in this book.

There can also be scepticism, or even hostility, when a group of oppressed people, such as women or disabled people, come together to write or carry out research. While writing a course on disability with other disabled people at the Open University, I have been asked whether it might not be 'rather subjective', and whether we might not have 'axes to grind'. In contrast, the copy editor, a disabled person herself, claims to have had the equivalent of a religious conversion while working on our text!

Spreading the word

As researchers and academics we need to write in prestigious journals in order to compete with our colleagues and receive kudos, promotion, or even the chance to change our jobs; we may, therefore, be motivated to reach the 'experts' rather than the public, and may sometimes be indifferent to the fact that very few people read or understand what we have written. In addition, those working under contract may be directed by their funders to publish in specific journals. The need to get material published can easily lead us to concentrate on journals sympathetic to our viewpoint resulting in knowledge being disseminated to a very specific audience, probably one that is already supportive of the opinions and ideas being raised. Academic journals have characteristic styles of presentation, as well as preferences for some research methodologies over others. By taking note of these factors, researchers and writers can make fairly accurate predictions of the likelihood of success in publishing their work; if they want to maximize their chances of success, and not waste valuable time, they are likely to study these points in some detail. There is nothing intrinsically wrong with this, but it can mean that their work reaches only a very specific group of people.

The popular versus the academic press

One meaning of the word 'publication' is 'to make generally known' (Fowler and Fowler 1964). Probably the best way of achieving this is to avoid prestigious journals, which few people read, and to concentrate instead on the popular press. Writing for the popular press is, however, unlikely to be encouraged in academic and professional circles. Roberts (1984) points out that having one's work described as 'journalistic' is rarely a compliment, and Shipman (1988) believes that prestige is as likely to be lost as gained through writing for popular publications.

Writing for the popular press can lead to other problems, mainly in terms of inappropriate editing and misrepresentation, usually in an attempt to 'catch the reader's eye' or to make a story more sensational. In the television programme *Link* (2 February 1992), for example, the negative impact which sensational articles about disability can have on disabled people was discussed. This gives rise to a considerable dilemma for researchers, for although the popular press is a more satisfactory way of disseminating research findings and ideas than academic journals, inasmuch as many more people read it, the knowledge is distorted and the writer tends to lose control. This point is illustrated below.

Roberts (1984) interviewed a sample of young working-class women in Bradford and concluded that they were not getting the same opportunities for advancement and success as young men. She sent her findings to a local newspaper in order to disseminate them to the research participants. She was alarmed when her research was given the title 'Bradford Girls Lack Drive' by the newspaper editor, as it totally misrepresented her conclusions. In contrast to this Roberts relates ways in which disseminating research findings to the popular press can be beneficial; for example when she sent her research findings on a numeracy course for women to a local newspaper, she received 500 letters from women asking for details of the course and giving considerable information about their difficulties with mathematics, information she used in a subsequent book. It is morally desirable to inform research participants of the ways in which research will be used and its likely repercussions but, when dealing with the popular press, this is not always possible.

I submitted an article to the newspaper *Therapy Weekly* in 1986 giving details of some research I had carried out on the attitudes of physiotherapists to the recruitment of disabled people into that profession (French 1986b). I mentioned in the article, almost in passing, that people who are very overweight were judged to be less suitable than people with various substantial disabilities. The title given to the article was, 'Obesity – A Greater Stigma than Disability' which certainly did not reflect its contents. In 1990 I submitted an article on the placebo effect to *Nursing Times*, where the main tenet of my argument was that the placebo effect is not magical but can be explained in terms of psychology and physiology (French 1990). Despite this, when I received the proofs, the title had been changed from 'The Powerful Placebo' to 'Magic Pills'. I felt strongly enough to wrangle over it with the editor, but to no avail. Despite these problems the information in these articles almost certainly reached more people than would have been the case if I had written for a more prestigious or academic journal, and perhaps the titles provided by the editors induced more people to read them than mine would have done.

Loss of control

When the research findings start to be disseminated, be it in the academic or the popular press, researchers lose all control of them. The findings may, over a period of time, be used in articles and books written by others where considerable pruning and reinterpretation may have taken place. The ideas may be taken out of context and used to support other theories or applied to areas not envisaged by the researcher. Shipman (1988) points out that Piaget did not apply his theory of child development to education, but it was, nonetheless, a major theory used in teacher training in the 1960s. The survival of evidence can become part of the mythology of a subject, even though the original research on which it is based is questionable or flawed. The use of information and ideas in diverse ways by different groups of people can, however, be highly creative.

Empowerment

There are, of course, many other ways of disseminating research material than by the printed word, such as giving talks at conferences or in the community. Feuerstein (1986) explains many ways of disseminating research findings, especially in the context of participatory research where some people may be unable to read. These methods include the use of photographs, pictures and films; cartoons can also be used to convey important information in a forceful way.

Greater flexibility and imagination over the dissemination of research material allows it to be shared by many more people and by people from diverse groups within society. Their feedback, in turn, is potentially of great value to researchers. Osborn and Willcocks (1990) believe, for example, that making research material accessible to older people can be politically powerful as it helps them to become actively involved in social change.

The power of the printed word

When any kind of material, including research findings, goes into print, it tends to be treated uncritically by many readers, particularly those who are not involved in research themselves. The published word gives ideas, opinions and research findings credibility and legitimacy, thereby bestowing on the researcher or author the status of 'expert'. Spender (1981) states, 'it would appear that some mysterious transformation occurs when the private becomes public and personal opinions are translated into print.'

Those of us who can write, or who have jumped various academic hurdles, are given the opportunity to share our ideas with researchers, professionals and the general public, even though we may not view ourselves as experts on the topic in question. At the very least, the high profile our ideas have, will mean that they impinge upon people's consciousness more than the ideas and opinions of others. Good writers quickly become well known and are invariably asked to write again and again; in that way their ideas can start to exert a powerful influence.

In 1989 I wrote four articles on 'teaching methods' which were published in the journal *Physiotherapy* (French 1989b, c, d, e). They were short, simple articles which were drawn from my own experiences and a few basic books. Since writing the articles I have been asked to run workshops on teaching methods; the articles have also been used as reading material on short courses, and they form the basis of a forthcoming book (French et al. in press). Yet I do not regard myself as an expert on the subject, but rather someone who, for inexplicable reasons, simply likes to write.

I have also found that whenever I write on a topic, people assume I am merely divulging the tip of my iceberg of knowledge when, in reality, I have written down just about all I know, and am often using the process of writing as a means of motivating myself to learn! Yet, in another sense, what they believe is near to the truth, for when I write I am merely revealing those parts of the story which I am 'allowed', or which I dare, to tell.

It is, however, impossible for us as researchers to know the extent to which our research or writings are being used, or how much they are affecting other people's thinking or behaviour, as little feedback is given. I discovered, quite by chance, that an article I had written querying the notion of independence for disabled people (French 1991b), is used as part of the selection process for rehabilitation workers.

Much research, rather than being inappropriately used, is never used at all. Major decisions are frequently made without any reference to research, and many research reports are never read. Organizations may sponsor research to improve their status or image or for other internal political manoeuvrings (Hadley 1987). In addition, many researchers are wary of disseminating their material to people who might distort it to make a political point (Richardson et al. 1990). Probably the most important reasons for failing to use research findings are lack of political will and lack of resources. The good fortune, or judgement, of being in the right place at the right time can also be very important.

Conclusion

It is no easy or straightforward task for researchers to decide what to tell once their data have been collected and analysed. More importantly, what is told is shaped by social and political forces – the biases of editors and reviewers, the topicality of issues, the desire for recognition or promotion, and the need for further sponsorship. This is not to deny that many researchers have more worthy aims, such as the exposure of discrimination and prejudice against marginalized groups of people within society.

Academic and professional writing is tied to and shaped by prestige and privilege. Appointment or promotion often depends on what research people have done, how many articles they have published in a given period of time and in which journals. One of my motivations to write was to fill that discouraging large blank page headed 'publications' on every application form that came my way. The need to publish can lead us as academics to compromise our scholarship in an attempt to write as many articles as possible in a given space of time, or to use the same material again and again in different guises.

There are many unresolved problems and contradictions in the processes whereby we 'tell' our research. The peer review system, of which many of us are a part, can destroy authors, but can also enhance their writing and spur them on to greater heights; the popular press can distort knowledge, but can also make it easy for people to assimilate; published research can be used in diverse ways, some destructive but others highly creative. However our research findings are presented and used, it is clear that they are tightly bound to social and political forces and that whatever research is done bears less than a perfect resemblance to what is eventually told.

References

Adams, J. (1984) Reminiscence in the geriatric ward: an undervalued resource, *Oral History*, 12(2), 54–9.

Alexander, H. A. (1991) Research rigour request (a letter), *Physiotherapy*, 7(6), 387.

Allen, K. R. (1989) *Single Women/Family Ties: Life Histories of Older Women*. London, Sage.

Ardener, E. (1975) Belief and the problem of women. In Ardener, S. (ed.) *Perceiving Women*. London, Malaby Press.

Atkinson, D. (1988) Research interviews with people with mental handicaps, *Mental Handicap Research*, 1(1), 75–90.

Atkinson, D. (1991) *Past Times*. Unpublished.

Atkinson, D. and Williams, F. (eds) (1990) *Know Me as I Am: An Anthology of Prose, Poetry and Art by People with Learning Difficulties*. London, Hodder and Stoughton.

Bair, D. (1990) *Simone de Beauvoir: A Biography*. London, Jonathan Cape.

Barron, D. (1990) Locked away: life in an institution. In Brechin, A. and Walmsley, J. (eds) *Making Connections: Reflecting on the Lives and Experiences of People with Learning Difficulties*. London, Hodder and Stoughton.

Becker, H. (1971) *Sociological Work*. London, The Penguin Press.

Bell, C. and Roberts, H. (eds) (1984) *Social Researching, Politics, Problems, Practice*. London, Routledge and Kegan Paul.

Bercovici, S. (1981) Qualitative methods and cultural perspectives in the study of de-institutionalisation. In Brunininks, R., Meyers, C., Sigford, B. and Lakin, C. (eds) *Deinstitutionalisation and Community Adjustment of Mentally Retarded People*. Monograph of the American Association on Mental Deficiency, No. 4.

Bernard, M. and Meade, K. (1993) *Women Come of Age: Perspectives on the Lives of Older Women*. London, Edward Arnold.

Blake, A. (1992) Review: Common knowledge, *The Higher*, 16 October, p. 27.

Bogdan, R. and Taylor, S. J. (1982) *Inside Out: The Social Meaning of Retardation*. Toronto, University of Toronto Press.

Booth, T. (1983) Residents' views, rights and institutional care. In Fisher, M. (ed.) *Speaking of Clients*. Social Services Monograph: Research in Practice. University of Sheffield.

Booth, T. (1988) *Developing Policy Research.* Aldershot, Avebury.

Booth, T. (1993) Obstacles to the development of user centred services. In Slater, R. and Johnson, J. (eds) *Ageing and Later Life.* London, Sage.

Borland, K. (1991) 'That's not what I said': interpretive conflict in oral narrative research. In Gluck, S. and Patai, D. (eds) *Women's Words: The Feminist Practice of Oral History.* London, Routledge.

Bornat, J. (1978) Home and work: a new context for trade union history, *Radical America*, 12(5), September–October, 53–69.

Bornat, J. (1980) An examination of the General Union of Textile Workers: 1880–1920. Unpublished PhD, University of Essex.

Bornat, J. (1989) Oral history as a social movement: reminiscence and older people, *Oral History*, 17(2), Autumn, 16–24.

Bornat, J. (1992) The communities of community publishing, *Oral History*, Autumn, 23–31.

Bornat, J. (1993) Life experience. In Bernard, M. and Meade, K. (eds) *Women Come of Age: Perspectives on the Lives of Older Women.* London, Edward Arnold.

Bornat, J. (n.d.) Exploring Living Memory: Photos and Issues. Unpublished.

Bowles, G. and Duelli Klein, R. (eds) (1983) *Theories of Women's Studies.* London, Routledge and Kegan Paul.

Bradley, C. and Peberdy, A. (1988) Reproductive decision making and the value of children: the Tolai of East New Britain. In McDowell, N. (ed.) *Reproductive Decision Making and the Value of Children in Rural Papua New Guinea.* Port Moresby, the Institute of Applied Social and Economic Research.

Brechin, A. and Swain, J. (1987) *Changing Relationships: Shared Action Planning with People with a Mental Handicap.* London, Harper and Row.

British Sociological Association (BSA) (1993) *Sociology. Special Issue: Auto/Biography in Sociology*, 27(1), 1–197.

Broad, W. and Wade, N. (1982) *Betrayers of the Truth: Fraud and Deceit in Science.* Oxford, Oxford University Press.

Burgess, R. G. (ed.) (1984) *The Research Process in Educational Settings.* London, Falmer Press.

CCCS (1981) *Unpopular Education: Schooling and Social Democracy in England since 1944.* London, Hutchinson.

CCCS (1982) *The Empire Strikes Back.* London, Hutchinson.

Campbell, A. (1989) *To Square with Genesis.* Polygon, Edinburgh University Press.

Campling, J. (ed.) (1981) *Images of Ourselves: Women with Disabilities Talking.* London, Routledge and Kegan Paul.

Carver, R. P. (1978) The case against statistical significance testing, *Harvard Education Review*, 48(3), 378–99.

CESSA (1992) *Inside Quality Assurance.* London, CESSA, University of North London, Newport Pagnell, The Information Design Unit.

Clarke, J. (1991) *New Times and Old Enemies: Essays on Cultural Studies and America.* London, Harper Collins.

Coleman, P. (1986) *Ageing and Reminiscence Processes: Social and Clinical Implications.* Chichester, John Wiley.

Coleman, P. (1993) Reminiscence in the study of ageing: the social significance of story. In Bornat, J. (ed.) *Reminiscence Reviewed: Achievements, Perspectives, Evaluations.* Buckingham, Open University Press.

The Concise Oxford Edition (1976) 6th edn. Oxford, Oxford University Press.

Cox, B. D., Blaxter, M. et al. (1987) *The Health and Lifestyle Survey.* Cambridge, The Health Promotion Research Trust.

Crick, M. (1992) Ali and me: an essay in Street Corner anthropology. In Okely, J. and Callaway, H. (eds) *Anthropology and Autobiography.* London, Routledge.

Dale, A., Arber, S. and Procter, M. (1988) *Doing Secondary Analysis*. London, Unwin Hyman.

Dean, J. and Foote Whyte, W. (1978) How do you know if the informant is telling the truth? In Bynner, J. and Stribley, K. M. (eds) *Social Research: Principles and Procedures*. London, Longman.

DHSS (1986) *Residential Homes – Guidance on Standards of Accommodation*. Circular LAC (86)1. London, HMSO.

DHSS and Welsh Office (1973) Local Authority Building Note No. 2. *Residential Accommodation for Elderly People*. London, HMSO.

Duelli Klein, R. (1983) How to do what we want to do: thoughts about feminist methodology. In Bowles, G. and Duelli Klein, R., *Theories of Women's Studies*. London, Routledge and Kegan Paul.

Edgerton, R. B. (1967) *The Cloak of Competence*. Berkeley, University of California Press.

Edgerton, R. B. (ed.) (1984) Introduction. In *Lives in Process: Mentally Retarded Adults in a Large City*, Monograph No. 6. Washington, DC, American Association on Mental Deficiency.

Ely M., Anzul, M., Friedman, T. et al. (1991) *Doing Qualitative Research: Circles Within Circles*. London, Falmer Press.

Enos, A. (1977). School of music and dance, *Gigibori*, 3(2), 1–7.

Epstein, A. L. (1969) *Land, Politics and Change among the Tolai of Papua New Guinea*. Canberra, Australian National University Press.

Etter-Lewis, G. (1991) Black women's life stories: reclaiming self in narrative texts. In Gluck, S. and Patai, D. (eds) *Women's Words: The Feminist Practice of Oral History*. London, Routledge.

Evans, M. (1992) The personal is social: biography and social research. Paper given at the *Auto/Biography in Sociology* Conference, University of Manchester, January.

Fennell, G., Emerson, R., Sidell, M. and Hague, A. (1981) *Day Centres for the Elderly in East Anglia*. Norwich, Norwich Centre for East Anglian Studies.

Ferrarotti, F. (1981) On the autonomy of the biographical method. In Bertaux, D. (ed.) *Biography and Society*. London, Sage.

Feuerstein, M. (1986) *Partners in Evaluation*. London, Macmillan.

Fielding, N. G. and Fielding, J. L. (1986) *Linking Data*. London, Sage.

Finch, J. (1984) It's great to have someone to talk to: the ethics and politics of interviewing women. In Bell, C. and Roberts, H. (eds) *Social Researching, Politics, Problems, Practice*. London, Routledge and Kegan Paul.

Flynn, M. C. (1986) Adults who are mentally handicapped as consumers: issues and guidelines for interviewing, *Journal of Mental Deficiency Research*, 30, 369–77.

Foot Whyte, W. (1955) *Methodological Appendix* Reprinted in DE304 Blocks 1–4 Offprints, Open University 1979. Milton Keynes, Open University Educational Enterprises.

Foster, H. (ed.) (1985) *Postmodern Culture*. London, Pluto Press.

Fowler, H. W. and Fowler, H. G. (eds) (1964) *The Concise Oxford Dictionary*. Oxford, Oxford University Press.

Fox, A. J. and Goldblatt, P. O. (1982) *Longitudinal Study: Socio-Demographic Mortality Differentials*. Series SLS, No. 1. London, HMSO.

French, S. (1986a) *Handicapped People in the Health and Caring Professions: Attitudes, Practices and Experiences*, unpublished MSc Dissertation. London, South Bank University.

French, S. (1986b) Obesity – a greater stigma than disability, *Therapy Weekly*, 13(17), 5–6.

French, S. (1987) Attitudes of physiotherapists to the recruitment of disabled and handicapped people into the physiotherapy profession, *Physiotherapy*, 73(7), 363–7.

French, S. (1988) How significant is statistical significance?, *Physiotherapy*, 74(6), 266–8.
French, S. (1989a) *Interviews with Disabled Physiotherapists*, On-going PhD research. London, South Bank University.
French, S. (1989b) Teaching methods: 1. The lecture, *Physiotherapy*, 75(9), 509–10.
French, S. (1989c) Teaching methods: 2. The discussion group, *Physiotherapy*, 75(10), 613–15.
French, S. (1989d) Teaching methods: 3. Student centred learning, *Physiotherapy*, 75(11), 678–80.
French, S. (1989e) Teaching Methods: 4. Adding interest to your teaching, *Physiotherapy*, 75(12), 741–43.
French, S. (1990) Magic pills, *Nursing Times*, 86(17), 28–30.
French, S. (1991a) Setting a record straight, *Therapy Weekly*, 18(1), 4.
French, S. (1991b) What's so great about 'Independence'?, *The New Beacon*, 75(886) 153–6.
French, S. (ed.) (1992a) *Physiotherapy: A Psychosocial Approach*. Oxford, Butterworth Heinemann.
French, S. (1992b) Researching disability: the way forward, *Disability and Rehabilitation*, 14(4), 183–6.
French, S., Laing, J. and Neville, S. (in press) *Teaching and Learning: A Guide for Therapists*. Oxford, Butterworth Heinemann.
Garfinkel, H. (1967) *Studies in Ethnomethodology*. Englewood Cliffs, NJ, Prentice Hall.
Gergen, K. J. and Gergen, M. M. (1991) Towards reflective methodologies. In Steier, F. (ed.) *Research and Reflexivity*. London, Sage.
Glaser, B. G. and Strauss, A. S. (1967) *The Discovery of Grounded Theory*. Chicago, IL, Aldine.
Gluck, S. B. and Patai, D. (eds) (1991) *Women's Words: The Feminist Practice of Oral History*. London, Routledge.
Goffman, E. (1959) *Presentation of Self in Everyday Life*. New York, Doubleday Anchor.
Goffman, E. (1963) *Stigma: Notes on the Management of Spoiled Identity*. Englewood Cliffs, NJ, Prentice Hall.
Goffman, E. (1976) The structure of remedial exchanges. In Harre, R. (ed.) *Life Sentences*. New York, John Wiley and Sons.
Gordon, R. (1978) Unequal exchange, *Research in Melanesia*, 3 and 4, 7–9.
Gough, I. (1979) *The Political Economy of the Welfare State*. London, Macmillan.
Graham, H. (1984) Surveying through stories. In Bell, C. and Roberts, H. (eds) *Social Researching, Politics, Problems, Practice*. London, Routledge and Kegan Paul.
Grele, R. (1991) *Envelopes of Sound: The Art of Oral History*, 2nd ed. New York, Praeger.
Grewal, S., Kay, J., Landor, L. et al. (eds) (1988) *Charting the Journey: Writings by Black and Third World Women*. London, Sheba Feminist Publishers.
Grice, P. (1975) Logic and conversation. In Cole, P. and Morgan, J. L. (eds) *Syntax and Semantics: Vol. 3. Speech Acts*. New York, Academic Press.
Hadley, R. (1987) Publish and be ignored; proselytize and be damned. In Wenger, G. C. (ed.) *The Research Relationship*. London, Allen and Unwin.
Hale, S. (1991) Feminist method, process and self-criticism: interviewing Sudanese women. In Gluck, S. and Patai, D. (eds) *Women's Words: The Feminist Practice of Oral History*. London, Routledge.
Hall, S. (1980) Thatcherism – a new stage?, *Marxism Today*, February, 26–8.
Hall Carpenter Archives (1989) Inventing Ourselves: Lesbian Life Stories. London, Routledge.
Hammersley, M. (1989) *The Dilemma of the Qualitative Method*. London, Routledge.
Hammersley, M. and Atkinson, P. (1983) *Ethnography: Principles in Practice*. London, Tavistock.

Hanmer J. and Leonard D. (1984) Negotiating the problem: the DHSS and research on violence in marriage. In Bell, C. and Roberts, H. (eds) *Social Researching, Politics, Problems, Practice*. London, Routledge and Kegan Paul.

Harding, S. (ed.) (1987) *Feminism and Methodology*. Milton Keynes, Open University Press.

Harland, R. (1987) *Superstructuralism*. London, Methuen.

Harris, P. (1986) *Designing and Reporting Experiments*. Milton Keynes, Open University Press.

Heron, J. (1981) Philosophical basis for a new paradigm. In Reason, P. and Rowan, J. (eds) *Human Inquiry*. Chichester, John Wiley and Sons.

Hewitt, J. P. and Stokes, R. (1975) Disclaimers, *American Sociological Review*, 40(1), 1–11.

Holman, B. (1987) Research from the underside, *British Journal of Social Work*, 17, 669 83

Hooks, B. (1982) *Ain't I a Woman? Black Women and Feminism*. London, Pluto Press.

Horton, R. (1974) African traditional thought and western science. In Wilson, B (ed.) *Rationality*. Oxford, Basil Blackwell.

How to become a Chartered Physiotherapist (1984) London, Chartered Society of Physiotherapy.

Jahoda, A., Markova, I. and Cattermole, M. (1988) Stigma and the self-concept of people with a mild mental handicap, *Journal of Mental Deficiency Research*, 32, 103–15.

Jewish Women in London Group (1989) *Generations of Memories: Voices of Jewish Women*. London, The Women's Press.

Johnson, N. (1992) Review: never again Britain 1945–51, *The Higher*, 16 October, p. 19.

Jorgensen, D. (1989) *Participant Observation: A Methodology for Human Studies*. Beverly Hills, CA, Sage.

Joseph, G. (1981) The incompatible menage a trois. Marxism, feminism and racism. In Sargent, L. (ed.) *Women and Revolution*. London, Pluto Press.

Jourard, S. (1971) *Self Disclosure. An Experimental Analysis of the Transparent Self*. New York, John Wiley.

Jules-Rossette, B. (1975) *African Apostles*. Ithaca, NY, Cornell University Press.

Junker, B. (1960) *Fieldwork*. Chicago, University of Chicago Press.

Kellaher, L., Peace, S. and Willcocks, D. (1990) Triangulating data. In Peace, S. (ed.) *Researching Social Gerontology: Concepts, Methods and Issues*. London, Sage Publications.

Kellaher, L., Peace, S., Weaver, T. and Willcocks, D. (1988) *Coming to Terms with the Private Sector*. CESSA, Polytechnic of North London Press.

Kornblum, W. (1989) Introduction. In Smith, C. D. and Kornblum, W. (eds) *In the Field: Readings in the Field Research Experience*. New York, Praeger.

Ladner, S. (1987) Introduction to tomorrow's tomorrow: the black woman. In Harding, S., *Feminism and Methodology*. Milton Keynes, Open University Press.

Lederman, R. (1986) The return of red woman. In Golde, P. (ed.) *Women in the Field*. London, University of California Press.

Leonard, P. (1979) Restructuring the welfare state, *Marxism Today*, December.

Link (1992) ITV Television, 2 February.

Lofland, J. and Lofland, L. H. (1984) *Analysing Social Settings: A Guide to Qualitative Observation and Analysis*. Belmont, CA, Wadsworth.

Lorde, A. (1984) *Sister Outsider: Essays and Speeches*. New York, Crossing Press.

Luxton, M. and Findlay, S. (1989) Is the everyday world problematic? Reflections on Smith's method of making sense of women's experience, *Studies in Political Economy*, (30), 183–96.

Mahoney, M. J. (1977) Publication prejudice: an experimental study of confirmatory bias in the peer review system, *Cognitive Therapy and Research*, 1, 167–75.

Malinowski, B. (1967) *A Diary in the Strict Sense of the Term*. London, Routledge and Kegan Paul.

McCall, G. and Simmons, J. (1969) *Issues in Participant Observation*. Reading, MA, Addison Wesley.

McCormack Steinmatz, A. (1991) Doing. In Ely, M. et al., *Doing Qualitative Research: Circles within Circles*. London, Falmer Press.

McDermott, K. (1987) In and out of the game: a case study of contract research. In Wenger, G. C. (ed.) *The Research Relationship*. London, Allen and Unwin.

McKnight, J. (1981) Professionalised service and disabling help. In Brechin A., Liddiard P. and Swain J. (eds) *Handicap in a Social World*. Sevenoaks, Hodder and Stoughton.

Miles, M. B. and Huberman A. M. (1984) *Qualitative Data Analysis: A Source Book of New Methods*. Beverly Hills, CA, Sage.

Millett, K. (1991) *The Loony Bin Trip*. London, Virago Press.

Mishler, E. (1986) *Research Interviewing*. Harvard, Harvard University Press.

Moore, H. (1988) *Feminism and Anthropology*. Cambridge, Polity Press.

Morris, J. (1991) *Pride Against Prejudice: Transforming Attitudes to Disability*. London, Women's Press.

Neville, S. and French, S. (1991) Clinical education: students' and clinical tutors' views, *Physiotherapy*, 77(5), 351–4.

Nicholson, L. (1990) *Feminism/Postmodernism*. London, Routledge.

Norris, A. D. (1986) *Reminiscence with Elderly People*. Oxford, Winslow Press.

Oakley, A. (1981) Interviewing women: a contradiction in terms. In Roberts, H. (ed.) *Doing Feminist Research*. London, Routledge and Kegan Paul.

Oakley, A. (1992) *The Secret Lives of Eleanor Jenkinson*. London, Harper Collins.

Offe, C. (1984) *Contradictions of the Welfare State*. London, Hutchinson.

Okely, J. (1992) Anthropology and autobiography: participatory experience and embodied knowledge. In Okely, J. and Callaway, H. (eds) *Anthropology and Autobiography*. London, Routledge.

Okely, J. and Callaway, H. (eds) (1992) *Anthropology and Autobiography*. London, Routledge.

Oliver, M. (1987) Re-defining disability: a challenge to research, *Research, Policy and Planning*, 5(1), 9–13.

Oliver, M. (1990) *The Politics of Disablement*. London, Macmillan.

O'Neill, J. (1975) *Making Sense Together: An Introduction to Wild Sociology*. London, Heinemann.

Osborn, A. and Willcocks, D. (1990) Making research useful and usable. In Peace, S.M. (ed.) *Researching Social Gerontology*. London, Sage.

Pahl, J. (1992) The impact of feminist research on community care policy. In Smith, R. and Harrison, L. (eds) *Community Care Research and Community Care Policy*. University of Bristol, School of Advanced Urban Studies.

Parry, A. (1991) Physiotherapy and methods of inquiry: conflict and reconciliation, *Physiotherapy*, 77(7), 435–8.

Passerini, L. (1989) Women's personal narratives: Myths, experiences, and emotions. In Personal Narratives Group (eds) *Interpreting Women's Lives: Feminist Theory and Personal Narratives*. Bloomington, IN, University of Indiana Press.

Passerini, L. (1990) Mythbiography in oral history. In Samuel, R. and Thompson, P. (eds) *The Myths We Live By*. London, Routledge.

Patai, D. (1991) US academics and third world women: is ethical research possible? In Gluck, S. B. and Patai, D. (eds) *Women's Words: The Feminist Practice of Oral History*. London, Routledge.

Peace, S. (ed.) (1990) *Researching Social Gerontology*. London, Sage.

Peace, S., Hall, J. and Hamblin, G. (1979) *The Quality of Life of the Elderly in Residential Care*. Research report No. 1. Survey Research Unit, Polytechnic of North London.

Peace, S., Hall, J. and Hamblin, G. (1981) The use of Bradburn's Affect Balance Scale with the elderly in residential care. Appendix B in Davies, B. and Knapp, M. (eds) *Old People's Homes and the Production of Welfare*. London, Routledge and Kegan Paul.

Peace, S., Kellaher, L. and Willcocks, D. (1982) *A Balanced Life: A Consumer Study of Life in 100 Local Authority Old People's Homes*. Research Report 13. CESSA, Polytechnic of North London.

Peace, S., Kellaher, L. and Phillips, D. (1986) *A Model of Residential Care: Secondary Analysis of data from 100 Old People's Homes*. Final report to ESRC, No. G00232019.

Pearce, B. W. and Chen, V. (1989) Ethnography as sermonic: the rhetorics of Clifford Geertz and James Clifford. In Simons, H. W. (ed.) *Rhetoric in Human Sciences*. London, Sage.

Peberdy, A. (1988) Ritual and power. In Furlong, M. (ed.) *Mirror to the Church*. London, SPCK.

Personal Narratives Group (1989) Origins, *Interpreting Women's Lives: Feminist Theory and Personal Narratives*. Bloomington, IN, University of Indiana Press.

Peshkin, A. (1985) Virtuous subjectivity: in the participant observer's I's. In Berg, D. N. and Smith, K. K. (eds) *Exploring Clinical Methods for Social Research*. Beverly Hills, CA, Sage.

Plummer, K. (1983) *Documents of Life*. London, Allen and Unwin.

Portelli, A. (1988) Uchronic dreams: working class memory and possible worlds, *Oral History*, 16(2), Autumn.

Potts, M. and Fido, R. (1991) *A Fit Person to Be Removed*. Plymouth, Northcote House.

Purtilo, R. (1984) *Health Professional/Patient Interaction*. Philadelphia, W. B. Saunders.

Rattansi, A. (1982) State education and the state of education: social democratic reform and the crisis, *Critical Social Policy*, 2(2), 81–8.

Ravn, I. (1991) What should guide reality construction? In Steier, F. (ed.) *Research and Reflexivity*. London, Sage.

Reason, P. and Rowan, J. (1981) On making sense. In Reason, P. and Rowan, J. (eds) *Human Inquiry*. Chichester, John Wiley and Sons.

Reiter, R. R. (1975) *Towards an Anthropology of Women*. New York Monthly Review Press.

Richardson, A., Jackson, C. and Sykes, W. (1990) *Taking Research Seriously. Social and Community Planning Research*. London, HMSO.

Richardson, B. (1992) *Physiotherapy*, 78(8), 642 (Book Review).

Roberts, H. (ed.) (1981) *Doing Feminist Research*. London, Routledge and Kegan Paul.

Roberts, H. (1984) Putting the show on the road: the dissemination of research findings. In Bell, C. and Roberts, H. (eds) *Social Researching, Politics, Problems, Practice*. London, Routledge and Kegan Paul.

Russell Bernard, H. (1988) *Research Methods in Cultural Anthropology*. London, Sage.

Ryle, G. (1949) *The Concept of Mind*. London, Hutchinson.

Salisbury, R. (1967) Pidgin's respectable past, *New Guinea*, 2(2), 44–8.

Salisbury, R. (1970) *Vunamami*. London, University of California Press.

Sassoon, A. S. (1992) Equality, difference, citizenship: the politics of daily life. Subjective authenticity, cultural specificity, individual and collective projects: intellectual work in Europe today, paper presented at the *British Sociological Association Conference* 'A New Europe'. University of Kent, April.

Saville, J. (1957) The welfare state: an historical approach. Reprinted in Butterworth, E. and Holman, R. (1975) *Social Welfare in Modern Britain*. London, Fontana.

Saxton, M. and Howe, F. (1988) *With Wings: An Anthology of Literature by Women with Disabilities*. London, Virago Press.

Sayers, J. (1982) *Biological Politics*. London, Tavistock.

Sayles, J. (1992) At the anarchists' convention. In *The Anarchists' Convention: Stories*. New York, Harper Collins.

Schön, D. (1990) *The Reflective Practitioner: How Professionals Think in Action*. Aldershot, Avebury.

Seldon, A. and Papworth, J. (1983) *By Word of Mouth: Elite Oral History*. London, Methuen.

Shipman, M. (1988) *The Limitations of Social research*, 3rd edn. London, Longman.

Sidell, M. (1991) *Gender Differences in the Health of Older Women*. Research Report, Milton Keynes, Department of Health and Social Welfare, The Open University.

Skyte, S. (1990) Understanding the media, *Physiotherapy*, 72(2), 693–4.

Smith, C. D. and Kornblum, W. (eds) (1989) *In the Field. Readings on the Field Research Experience*. New York, Praeger.

Smith, D. E. (1978) A peculiar eclipsing: women's exclusion from man's culture, *International Quarterly*, 1(4), 281–96.

Smith, D. E. (1987) *The Everyday World as Problematic*. Toronto, University of Toronto Press.

Smith, D. E. (1988) Women's perspective as a radical critique of sociology. In Harding, S. (ed.) *Feminism and Methodology*. Milton Keynes, Open University Press.

Smith, D. E. (1989) Feminist reflections on political economy, *Studies in Political Economy*, 30, 37–59.

Social Research Association (1992/93) *Social Research Association Ethical Guidelines*. Social Research Association Directory of Members, 1992/1993.

Soderqvist, T. (1991) Biography or ethnobiography or both? Embodied reflexivity and the deconstruction of knowledge power. In Steier, F. (ed.) *Research and Reflexivity*. London, Sage.

Spender, D. (1981) The gatekeepers: a feminist critique of academic publishing. In Roberts H. (ed.) *Doing Feminist Research*. London, Routledge and Kegan Paul.

Spender, D. (1985) *Man Made Language*, 2nd edn. London, Routledge and Kegan Paul.

Spindler, G. and L. (1971) Fieldwork among the Menomini. In Spindler, G. (ed.) *Being an Anthropologist: Fieldwork in Eleven Cultures*. New York, Holt, Rinehart and Winston.

Stacey, J. (1990) *Brave New Families: Stories of Domestic Upheaval in Late Twentieth Century America*. USA, Basic Books.

Stacey, J. (1991) Can there be a feminist ethnography? In Gluck, S. and Patai, D. (eds) *Women's Words: The Feminist Practice of Oral History*. London, Routledge.

Stanley, L. (1992) *The Auto/Biographical I: The Theory and Practice of Feminist Auto/ Biography*. Manchester, Manchester University Press.

Stanley, L. and Wise, S. (1983a) Back into the persona or: our attempt to construct feminist research. In Bowles, G. and Duelli Klein, R. (eds) *Theories of Women's Studies*. London, Routledge and Kegan Paul.

Stanley, L. and Wise, S. (1983b) *Breaking Out: Feminist Consciousness and Feminist Research*. London, Routledge and Kegan Paul.

Steier, F. (ed.) (1991) *Research and Reflexivity*. London, Sage.

Steier, F. (1991) Research as self-reflexivity, self-reflexivity as social process. In Steier, F. (ed.) *Research and Reflexivity*. London, Sage.

Stone, S. (1991) Qualitative research methods for physiotherapists, *Physiotherapy*, 77(7), 449–52.

Sutcliffe, J. and Simons, K. (1993) *Self-Advocacy and Adults with Learning Disabilities: Contexts and Debates*. Leicester, NIACE.

Swain, J., Finkelstein, V., French, S. and Oliver, M. (eds) (1993) *Disabling Barriers – Enabling Environments*. London, Sage.

Taylor, G. and Bishop, J. (eds) (1991) *Being Deaf: The Meaning of Deafness*. London, Pinter Publishers.

The Open University (1993) *Community Care. K259*. Milton Keynes, The Open University.

Thompson, P. (1978) *The Voice of the Past*, 1st edn. Oxford, Oxford University Press.

Thompson, P. (1988) *The Voice of the Past*, 2nd edn. Oxford, Oxford University Press.

Thornton Dill, B. (1988) The dialectics of black womanhood. In Harding, S. (ed.) *Feminism and Methodology*. Milton Keynes, Open University Press.

Walford, G. (ed.) (1991) *Doing Education Research*. London, Routledge.

Walmsley, J. (1989) The meaning of adulthood in the lives of some people with learning difficulties, unpublished MSC dissertation. Milton Keynes, The Open University.

Walmsley, J. (in progress) *People with Learning Difficulties: Experiences of Care and Caring*. PhD thesis, Milton Keynes, The Open University.

Wedderburn, D. (1965) Facts and theories of the welfare state. In Miliband, R. and Saville, J. (eds) *The Socialist Register*. London, Merlin Press.

Weedon, C. (1987) *Feminist Practice and Poststructuralist Theory*. Oxford, Basil Blackwell.

Wenger, G. C. (1987) *The Research Relationship: Practice and Politics in Social Policy Research*. London, Allen and Unwin.

Wilkinson, J. (1990) Being there: a way to evaluate life quality, starting with a person's feelings and daily experience. In Brechin, A. and Walmsley, J. (eds) *Making Connections*. London, Hodder and Stoughton.

Willcocks, D., Peace, S. and Kellaher, L. (1987) *Private Lives in Public Places: A Research-Based Critique of Residential Life in Local Authority Old People's Homes*. London, Tavistock.

Williams, F. (1987) 'Race', racism and the discipline of social policy: a critique, *Critical Social Policy*, (20), 4–29.

Williams, F. (1989a) *Social Policy: A Critical Introduction. Issues of Race, Gender and Class*. Cambridge, Polity Press.

Williams, F. (1989b) Mental handicap and oppression. In Brechin, A. and Walmsley, J. (eds) *Making Connections*. Sevenoaks, Hodder and Stoughton.

Williams, F. (1992a) Women with learning difficulties are women, too. In Langan, M. and Day, L. (eds) *Women, Oppression and Social Work*. London, Routledge.

Williams, F. (1992b) Somewhere over the rainbow: universality and diversity in social policy. In Manning, N. and Page, R. (eds) *Social Policy Review 4*. Canterbury, Social Policy Association.

Williams, F. (1992c) Women and community. In Bornat, J., Pereira, C., Pilgrim, D. and Williams, F., *Community Care: A Reader*. London, Macmillan.

Williams, F. (1993a) Gender, race and class in British welfare policy. In Clarke, J. and Cochrane, A. (eds) *Issues in Social Policy: the United Kingdom in International Context*. London, Sage.

Williams, F. (1993b) Social relations, welfare and the post-Fordism debate. In Burrows, R. and Loader, B. (eds) *Towards a Post-Fordist Welfare State*. London, Routledge.

Williams, P. and Schoultz, B. (1982) *We can Speak for Ourselves: Self-advocacy by Mentally Handicapped People*. London, Souvenir Press.

Wolf, C. (1987) *The Fourth Dimension: Interviews with Christa Wolf*. London, Verso.

Woodberry Down Memories Group (1989) *Woodberry Down Memories: The History of an LCC Housing Estate*. London, ILEA/EdROP.

Woolfe, V. (1977) *A Room of One's Own*. St Albans, Granada Publishing Ltd (first published 1929).

World Health Organization (1976) *Final Report of the First Regional Group on Basic Health Services*. Manilla, WHO Regional Office.

Writing for physiotherapy: guide lines for authors (1991) *Physiotherapy*, 77 (11), 769–70.

Index

DOING YOUR RESEARCH PROJECT (2nd edition)
A GUIDE FOR FIRST-TIME RESEARCHERS IN EDUCATION AND SOCIAL SCIENCE

Judith Bell

If you are a beginner researcher, the problems facing you are much the same whether you are producing a small project, an MEd dissertation or a PhD thesis. You will need to select a topic; identify the objectives of your study; plan and design a suitable methodology; devise research instruments; negotiate access to institutions, material and people; collect, analyse and present information; and finally, produce a well-written report or dissertation. Whatever the scale of the undertaking, you will have to master techniques and devise a plan of action which does not attempt more than the limitations of expertise, time and access permit.

We all learn to do research by actually doing it, but a great deal of time can be wasted and goodwill dissipated by inadequate preparation. This book aims to provide you with the tools to do the job, to help you avoid some of the pitfalls and time-wasting false trails that can eat into your time, to establish good research habits, and to take you from the stage of choosing a topic through to the production of a well-planned, methodologically sound and well-written final report or dissertation on time.

Doing Your Research Project serves as a source of reference and guide to good practice for all beginner researchers, whether undergraduate and postgraduate students or professionals such as teachers or social workers undertaking investigations in Education and the Social Sciences. This second edition retains the basic structure of the very successful first edition whilst incorporating some important new material.

Contents
Introduction – Approaches to educational research – Planning the project – Keeping records and making notes – Reviewing the literature – Negotiating access and the problems of inside research – The analysis of documentary evidence – Designing and administering questionnaires – Planning and conducting interviews – Diaries – Observation studies – Interpretation and presentation of the evidence – Postscript – References – Index.

192pp   0 335 19094 4 (Paperback)

CULTURAL POLITICS IN EVERYDAY LIFE
SOCIAL CONSTRUCTIONISM, RHETORIC AND KNOWING OF THE THIRD KIND

John Shotter

John Shotter argues that it is not in the writings of philosophers, sociologists or other 'theorists' that we can find the basis for what to do for the best in our lives; our judgments can only be rooted in the 'hurly burly' of the everyday, civil life of society. Ordinary people in their conversations and in their practical knowledge create the basic reality in which social institutions have their life. In setting out his social constructionist view of everyday life, Shotter draws in the work of Bakhtin, Billig, Gergen, Harré, MacIntyre, Rorty, Vico Volosinov, Vygotsky and Wittgenstein; and he connects such 'theoretical' and 'foundations' topics as 'realism' and 'foundations' to social concerns such as rights, citizenship and access to public debate. He is concerned with human culture in the widest sense, with ideas of personal relationships, civil society, social ecology, identity and belonging. *Cultural Politics of Everyday Life* is an important contribution to debates in social and cultural theory.

> In this extremely erudite book, John Shotter constructs a series of interlocking arguments about the nature of knowledge which we use in everyday life . . . *Cultural Politics of Everyday Life* is an important and deeply thoughtful examination of social constructionism's basic presuppositions.
>
> (Professor Michael Billig)

> This is a book to ponder, not to skim. Consistent with its own commitments, it invites argument on many levels. Complex and challenging, *Cultural Politics of Everyday Life* will richly reward those interested in the intellectual history of the most distinctive of contemporary social theories, 'social constructionism'.
>
> (Professor W. Barnett Pearce)

Contents

256pp   0 335 19120 7 (Paperback)   0 335 09762 6 (Hardback)

Not available from Open University Press in North America

FEMINISM AND METHODOLOGY
SOCIAL SCIENCE ISSUES

Sandra Harding (ed.)

Appearing in the feminist social science literature from its beginnings are a series of questions about methodology. In this collection, Sandra Harding interrogates some of the classic essays from the last fifteen years in order to explore the basic and troubling questions about science and social experience, gender, and politics.

Some of the essays report the uses of familiar research techniques to answer new questions or to rethink old ones. Some borrow concepts and theories from one field to illuminate another. All bring into focus new issues about social relations between women and men, about the causes and consequences of social change and social stability, about our sexual identities, and about the obscuring effects of culturewide gender symbolisms. They also reveal serious problems with assumptions about scientific method in the existing social science and philosophy literature. This collection provides a valuable introduction to the crucial methodological and epistemological issues feminist inquiry raises for scholars in all fields. *Feminism and Methodology* will be useful as a text in undergraduate and graduate history, social science, philosophy, and women's studies courses.

Contents

Contributors
Carol Gilligan, Sandra Harding, Heidi I. Hartmann, Nancy C. M. Hartsock, Joan Kelly-Gadol, Joyce A. Ladner, Catharine A. MacKinnon, Marcia Millman, Rosabeth Moss Kanter, Dorothy E. Smith, Bonnie Thornton Dill, Carolyn Wood Sherif.

208pp   0 335 15560 X (Paperback)   0 335 15561 8 (Hardback)

Not available from Open University Press in North America

X